Life's *Ultimate Questions:*

EXPLORING THE STORIES THAT SHAPE OUR EVERYDAY

JAKE WIENS

 FriesenPress

Suite 300 - 990 Fort St
Victoria, BC, V8V 3K2
Canada

www.friesenpress.com

ISBN
978-1-4602-8962-4 (Hardcover)
978-1-4602-8963-1 (Paperback)
978-1-4602-8964-8 (eBook)

1. RELIGION, CHRISTIAN EDUCATION

*What is truth, Evil and suffering, Higher power, Religious
literacy, Faith journey, Humanism, Body, soul and spirit*

Distributed to the trade by The Ingram Book Company

Table of Contents

Socrates, "The unexamined life is not worth living."

Jesus, "You will know the truth and the truth will set you free."
John 8:32

May, 2017   Prince George, British Columbia

to BSW who has stepped aside

and

to the graduating class of 2014
Cedars Christian School (CCS)

Prince George, British Columbia

VIII

Ancient Forest Provincial Park (McBride, British Columbia) Photograph, Chris Harris.

The Metaphor in the Cover Photo

This photo, it seemed to me, was an excellent metaphor for the faith-journey we are taking.

This is how my mind processed the two: Who would have expected a rainforest here, so many miles from the coast? (Surprised by truth!) The giant trees, witnesses to our journey, the well-marked path through the wilderness whose destination is as yet invisible, the path not too wide but wide enough for a friend or two, a pathway built for all, disabled and able-bodied, young and old alike. The pathway has its twists and turns, but you won't get lost. I'll let you take these thoughts to the next stage.

Notes and Credits

All biblical references are NIV-New International Version.

Chapter division drawings by Elise Everard, CCS grad, 2016.

Earth-from-Space photograph page 196, Hubble Space Telescope's Ultra Deep Field page 252, courtesy of NASA.

Thank you to Debbie Van Calsteren who took my too-expressive journaling to a higher literary level.

Preface

This was never meant to be a book. I was just writing, really just journaling to help me process my own challenges along life's faith journey.
Looking back I see the many questions, the many times I had lost my
way. What helped me find the path again? What kept me plodding on
when the light seemed so dim? My journaling helped me keep my head
above the waters; helped me refocus on the distant shore and it helped
me find the life rafts that were available.

Having dedicated my career to helping young people find this path
that does lead to life, that does give strength in the storms that threaten
to overwhelm, it was only logical to try to apply the lessons that I was
learning. How can my generation help the one following? What enables
some to thrive as true disciples of Jesus Christ as they leave the protective environment of home, church and / or Christian School? What was
lacking for the many who stumbled? What enables some to return at a
later date?

My journaling birthed into a booklet when I encountered the Bible's
overarching cosmic story in a radically new way; no longer just a series
of stories, no longer a book of mini-devotionals and lesson plans but a
Kingdom Story that grabbed the imagination and touched the heart in a
deeper way. This WOW experience provided the energy and the passion
needed to embark on this new writing path. How many of our young
people, how many of my own generation, are missing out because they
lack a piece of the puzzle, the piece that completes the whole?

Having to process life as curriculum, it was only natural for me to
think of all the related questions to these concerns. The attempt at organizing my many journal entries led to the discovery of the five compli-
mentary themes. This fivefold foundation formed the backbone of this

endeavor. No longer a booklet, it has now become a book that seems to promise encouragement for fellow travellers needing to gain more confidence for the faith journey.

As I read and reread this book I do recognize the many growth experiences of my last several decades. This book is, to a large part, the product of the many opportunities that my career at Cedars Christian School provided me. I am so very grateful to this wonderful community of faith where robust learning and a reaching for a higher bar was a way of life for students and staff alike.

I am thankful for the many 24/7 class trips I made as a teacher. These experiences repeatedly caused me to process the bigger issues of life with young people embarking on life's journey. Thanks to these teens (now young adults) who encouraged me to think more deeply.

All of these school trips were to cross cultural settings, either to the slums of Northern Mexico or to Eastside Vancouver, Canada's poorest postal code (sponsored by Youth with a Mission). In such cross-cultural settings one does learn to look more critically and hopefully more constructively at one's own culture and subculture. This increased sensitivity to the blind spots in one's community, and hopefully also to those in our own personal lives, is such a critical first step in any growth.

This book is offered to fellow travellers, particularly young adults who are struggling to make sense of life and faith in the context of a very challenging culture. This book is offered with the prayer that God the Spirit would provide fellow travellers with the WOW encounters with truth that do put it sufficiently together to enable a more confident moving forward on life's faith journey.

My journaling has morphed into a "travel guide" for young people leaving home, leaving high school. Too many are adding "Leaving the church, leaving the faith" to that list as well. My goal has been to encourage these young people, our leaders of tomorrow, the parents of tomorrow, to take care so that the faith issues do not get lost in all the packing and leaving and the setting up of new pads all their own.

Credits and references as needed are included in the sidebars. To be sure everything in this book is "borrowed" from spiritual giants I have encountered along my pathway. These spiritual giants are listed in the Reading List provided at the end. Many remain anonymous because there are simply too-many-to-name who have helped me along my faith journey and all of its detours.

I invite you to a blog to help in group discussions of the topics raised in this book.

Go to – **https://lifesultimatequestions.blogspot.com**
To post you will need to sign in through a Google account.

Life's Ultimate Questions, the "Why" of this Book

These questions may very well be the human heart's last frontier – and may remain so for everyone's personal journey towards self-understanding and for arriving at a state of inner peace with one's personal universe.

- The Question of Truth – The Foundational Question.
    - What is truth, and how can we validate it as true?
    - Is there a Higher Power, if so, what are the dynamics of our relationship with 'Him'?

- The Questions Surrounding our Humanity.
    - What does it mean to be human?
    - What is the purpose of our lives?

- The Question of Ethics.
    - What are life-enhancing behaviors?
    - How do we unwrap our sexuality, this greatest of personality gifts, so that it is life-giving rather than life-destroying?

- The Questions Surrounding Evil and Suffering.
    - Where does evil come from?
    - Why is suffering and loss so universal?
    - What is the solution to the seemingly universal human tendency towards evil?

- The Questions Surrounding the Future.
  - ◻ What happens to us after death?
  - ◻ How does the cosmic story end?
  - ◻ What gives us hope, sufficient to help us survive in the most challenging of situations?

The few observations about these questions that became the inspiration for this book:

1. These may very well be the most important questions of our lifetime. Our answers invariably shape our day to day as well as our destiny.

2. Possibly only a few have developed the awareness as to how they came to develop their answers to these questions.

3. Possibly fewer still would be able to give good reasons for the answers they have.

4. Possibly only a few have explored these questions thoroughly and most of these few, possibly only during times of crisis.

Based on these four observations, an exploration of these themes may very well be the most important journey anyone can take.

The best way to explore this book is to see it as a journey for a seeker after truth. In our day, so many have walked away, or are just slipping away, from a superficial encounter with the Biblical Story. Many others may never have considered faith issues to any degree. The search for truths to live by continues to beckon. How do we begin? This book suggests a five-fold pathway, five themes that together should be able to provide a sure foundation for a more confident and authentic faith experience within the context of our shallow, materialistic, rationalistic, and (many would say) twisted culture. Every young person, every new believer needs such a multifaceted foundation so as to stay the course and arrive safely at *Life's* destination – whatever that may be.

Part 1 – Recapturing the value of a spiritual quest. We need to come to the deeper realization that our lives are so much more than a superficial coming and going within the physical and social dimension.

Part 2 – Cultural roadblocks need to be examined. Our culture's decades-long avoidance of all topics related to religion and the current hyper-emotional reactions created by religious extremism from so many fronts have created not only an informational (and mis-informational) vacuum but also emotional blockages that need to be addressed.

Part 3 – Basic religious literacy. We should look at the various religions to see that each is really a cosmic story from the beginning to the end of time. Evolutionary atheism, also known as secular humanism, has such a cosmic story as well. This story must be seen as the religion or "unreligion" of our modern cultures. Each of these cosmic stories in its own way answers Life's Ultimate Questions. Every human being has such a story (maybe subconscious, unknown, unexamined) for his / her own set of answers. Possibly everyone should be considered "religious" at the core.

Part 4 – Exposing and validating our foundational assumptions. We need to explore the process as to how to critique and validate one's own faith; the "rational story" layer that supports our answers to Life's Ultimate Questions.

Part 5 – Encountering the Bible's overarching Mother-Story. This may ignite or reignite the imagination and the passion to participate more wholeheartedly in this cosmic story that promises so much, and is able to satisfy so deeply, even as we wait for the fulfillment of all that was prophetically anticipated right from its very beginning.

PATHWAY TO CONFIDENCE

1. *Empowering Spirituality*

2. Cultural Awareness

3. Religious Literacy

4. Validating our Faith Assumptions

5. Encountering the Kingdom Story

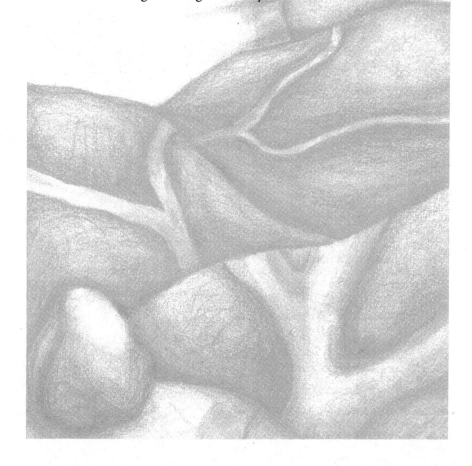

Part 1: Empowering Spirituality

a few thoughts to begin with...

Spirituality is one of the new buzzwords in our culture. Interestingly it has become an empty word that everyone can fill as they wish.

What is spirituality as it has been understood through the ages?

We are all part of larger stories than the simple one that begins with birth and ends with death. We are all part of our family's and our ethnic people-group's stories. As Canadians we are all participants in our country's story. Most importantly, as a member of the human family we are part of the human story. To understand this larger human story is the burden of religion. How to be a meaningful and active participant in one's inherited or adopted human story is the burden of spirituality.

There are five basic interpretations for the human story, with many variations in keeping with the five key perspectives for God, the main character in the stories ('no-god' is one of these five). You and I, by default, because we are human, are participants in one of these stories.

Is this at all important? For any journey to be successful it needs to be carefully planned. For a life to be well lived, the stories in which we participate need to be understood. This is life's greatest challenge and the burden that each generation has for the next. The fact that much of the human story is shrouded in mystery, and as a result controversy, should encourage us all to walk and reflect with even greater care, rather than to simply blow it away in mindless and mind-numbing ways. Our lives are priceless and we live the story only once.

This first section seeks to explore spirituality from the perspective of the Judeo-Christian tradition. A reader who is or has struggled to make Christianity "work" in the day to day may find this section helpful. Others who are on a different section of life's journey may want to read all or parts of this first section after reading the rest of the book.

The Promise of a Spiritual Quest

Virtually all cultures have had well developed concepts for spiritual quests. Often this quest has been associated with coming of age rituals. These quests may be revisited throughout life as pilgrimage. End of life crisis creates the context for such quests as well.

Often these quests were associated with specific holy places, often seen as spiritual hotspots. At other times, these quests were a retreating into the calmness of nature. These quests could have been as individuals or in groups. Sometimes they were associated with spiritual guides and with rituals. The focus was to reconnect with the spiritual dimension.

There seemed to be a universal longing to connect with something bigger that seemed to be beyond us, or as some suggested, something deep within us. There was the deeper sense that there was mystery within the universe, and this mystery was somehow the key to our existence. This led to mysticism, and the varied practices of the mystics can be observed across all cultures. When associated with the youth to adult rites of passage, communities considered such a quest and the discovery of at least a degree of the mystery essential for success in life. At other times it may have been associated with a deep felt need for refocusing, for reprioritizing, possibly for inner healing or reenergizing. Such a quest was considered the key for the successful transition into the afterlife, the mystery that eclipses all other mysteries.

Spiritual quests, pilgrimages, and rites of passage seem to have all gone by the wayside in our modern western cultures.

- Have we become too busy? Are we having too much fun?

- Has the "blessing" of a materially abundant lifestyle drowned out these "silly notions" of some invisible dimension?
- Has the pursuit of higher education replaced such a heart-learning quest?
- Have these spiritual traditions all gone by the wayside because our scientific understanding of the universe has eliminated the mystery, and with it the need for God, as well as the whole notion of a spiritual dimension?
- Have we finally evolved out of the "psychotic neurosis" that is suggested by these antiquated spiritual concepts?
- Possibly our culture has simply replaced all of this "silliness of a spiritual quest" with the tangible realities of turning sixteen, getting driver's licenses, or nineteen (that first legal beer) or graduation from grade 12, or the first kiss, or the first time!
- And for those later in life, not a spiritual pilgrimage, but as Hollywood would suggest, the personal bucket list.

However we look at it, the question refuses to die; have we lost something significant along the way?

To begin with we need to explore what is meant by the spiritual. Increasingly people are beginning to awaken to the need to go deeper rather than simply to pursue what is available at the shopping malls, stadiums, and theatres of our culture. For many even the superficiality of "churchianity – a tradition only" seems inadequate. Spirituality is becoming a regular theme on the menu for many career as well as life-related workshops.

BODY, SOUL (THE SELF), AND SPIRIT

To help us understand the spiritual, we need to explore these three interconnected and interdependent dimensions of our humanity. All religions suggest these three dimensions for an adequate self-understanding.

What is included in each of these dimensions? What needs are suggested by each? How do we seek to meet those needs?

A good exercise would be to brainstorm alone or as a group. Divide the white board into three columns and create your lists. Several things should become immediately apparent. Given our culture's fixation on the physical, we should have no problem filling in the BODY column. We may find the SOUL column more challenging. Possibly we would have great difficulty listing even a few items in the SPIRIT column. It may seem like the great unknown.

Second, we may struggle with some items, not really knowing in which column they belong. This would suggest that the lines between the columns are broken lines. The three overlap to a large degree. They are very much interdependent and interrelated. Some items may even seem to belong in more than one column. The health, or lack thereof, of one of the columns has huge implications for the other two. We are indeed complex creatures! There is mystery even here. We are more than highly evolved animals, or complex bundles of chemistry.

Body	Soul	Spirit
Food	Friendship	?????
Creature comforts – warmth, softness	Soul-Mate	
Drink	Sex?	
Alcohol	Touch?	
Health	Music	
Fitness	Art	
Sex	Belonging	
Touch	Community	
Body Art – Jewelry, tattoos, muscle sculpting		
Fashion		
Sweet / savory treats		
Music ? – the beat !		

A simple way of processing these columns is to recognize that it is the body that allows us to enjoy the physical world around us. The soul enables us to enjoy each other, (and our personality-rich pets as well). The spirit enables us to connect with the mystery in our environment, in our relationships, and with God. The "us" in all these statements refers to the soul. This "self" enjoys the gateway provided by the body, seeks to connect with other souls, and wonders about the spiritual and the mystery that is suggested therein.

Another help is to see plants as body: just chemistry, biology, physics. The animal world has body as well as soul. We do notice emotions within animals as well as relationships between animals. But it is humanity that has all three: body, soul and spirit. It is only humanity that asks questions with respect to meaning and purpose. It is only we who wonder about our existence and who seek connection with the mystery beyond. It is only humans who look at the panorama of a star-lit night sky and ask, "Are we alone in the cosmos? Is there meaning in or beyond the stars?"

WHAT BELONGS IN THE SPIRIT COLUMN?

There may be some debate as to where the dotted lines should be, whether more to the left or more to the right. As a general rule of thumb I have used the following guideline; the degree that these realities are mysterious, to that degree that item (also) belongs in the SPIRIT column.

The mystery in our relationships – Other people, to a degree are beyond our control, they are, to a degree, a mystery to us. The following spiritual qualities help us process this uncertainty constructively:

> The ability to forgive others: "To err is human, to forgive divine." Alexander Pope

> The ability to receive forgiveness from others, to experience restoration of relationship.

The ability to love others unconditionally, without needing to change or control them; to love them simply because they too need unconditional love.

Experiencing unconditional acceptance; being completely vulnerable but still enjoying wholesome acceptance.

The mystery within myself – to a degree I do not even know myself.

The ability to accept myself just as I am. "A curious paradox indeed, when I begin to accept myself just as I am, that is when I can change." Carl Rogers

The ability to forgive myself for my own personal mistakes that may have shipwrecked a part of my life.

Having purpose for my life – something to live for, worth dying for.

Search for significance, being a blessing, leaving a legacy.

Contentment – freedom from the addiction of always needing "more" (Do we not all struggle with our own set of addictions?)

Guidance – what do I do with my life, so many choices but at a loss which to choose.

Inner strength, wholeness, peace, the foundation for making the most out of the "basket" that life has handed me.

The mystery in my uncertain circumstances

Attitude of thankfulness no matter what my circumstances; responding to life positively, seeing the possibilities rather than the reverse.

Hope – makes any struggle worth surviving; without it the smallest roadblock can cause some to check out.

Shalom – harmony; at peace within one's self, with one's environment at all levels of existence.

The mystery beyond

Fear of death, from acceptance of this universal reality to the realization that it might be more like a doorway to the fullness of all that seems so much like a "broken promise" on this side.

A Someone, a something, possibly some principle, some all-encompassing truth that enables me to make some sense of the wonder, the order, the beauty within creation and at the same time provide some help in processing the pain, the struggle, and the chaos of life.

A Someone who fills the emptiness, the loneliness within.

A Someone to worship, someone larger, more permanent, more significant than I. Do we secretly harbor the longing to have a friend larger than life itself? This may be more than the nostalgia of childhood dreams, or the superhero themes of so much popular literature.

A Someone who is able to supply what seems to be missing within. So often life presents us with challenges that seem so much beyond anything we could possibly handle on our own. The spiritual dimension seems to have within it the promise to supply what is lacking.

A growing realization that we are less like a pool, needing to carefully ration limited inner resources, and more like a channel that has found a source that never runs dry.

Observations

To read through such a list slowly, thoughtfully, possibly even prayerfully, is to awaken longings deep within, longings that may have been buried beneath the struggles and distractions of life. Just to read through such a list is to awaken hope that things may yet be able to change. It may indeed be possible to arrive at a confident moving forward with an infusion from the SPIRIT column. It may be necessary to limit the overpowering demands of the BODY to allow an enlivening within the SPIRIT column.

These observations are the energy that gives birth to the realization that a personal spiritual quest may indeed be the doorway to new beginnings.

A spiritual quest contains the promise that my life may yet be transformed...

From simply surviving to thriving
From simply going through the motions to life with passion
From being a drain on others to being a blessing to them
From feeling forever drained to springs of
living water flowing from within
From feeling disconnected to having an holistic centre
From hoarding inner resources to overflowing with abundance
From life stressed to living above the circumstances

From feeling lost to having a sense of direction
From lives of quiet desperation to lives of hopeful expectations
From dragging one's feet to being carried on eagles' wings

From merely a short-lived spiritual quest to a New Way of Living
The SOUL enhanced or in today's lingo "the SOUL on steroids"

All of these transformations happen from one degree to the next, a growing into, the deeper the spiritual root, the greater the blessing.

There lies tremendous promise in such a quest. The first of the Beatitudes from Jesus' Sermon on the Mount, the foundation of all nine beatitudes, as well as the whole Sermon on the Mount, simply states

"Blessed are the poor in spirit for theirs is the
Kingdom of Heaven." Matthew 5:3

To paraphrase the truth that is contained here; blessed are those people who recognize their personal poverty of spirit (lack within the SPIRIT column). They have come to recognize that this lack is foundational to their very existence. They recognize that this lack, if not satisfied will result in a life that will miss out on the most important dimension of what it means to be human.

The promise is added; they will experience the blessing; they will inherit the Kingdom of Heaven. They will receive the life that could be characterized as Kingdom Living for time... and for eternity.

The Dilemma Inherent in a Spiritual Quest

A spiritual quest is all about connecting with the spiritual dimension. That dimension is a mystery, new territory for all of us. The God who resides in that dimension is more mysterious still, essentially unknowable by us finite as well as sinful people. How challenging, if not hopeless, our quest to enter into his presence, to tap into his life-giving power! God, by any stretch of the imagination, is simply past finding out.

Our spiritual quest may seem doomed before it even begins. But before we give up, let's consider the lessons learned by others more desperate than you or I.

Alcoholics Anonymous (AA) has popularized, maybe even coined the term "the God of our understanding." This suggests that all of us begin our search for God with a very limited, probably even an erroneous understanding of who this God really is. But like every drunk, whose very last hope is totally dependent on finding this higher power in this unknown dimension, so too we must begin where we are. We begin our search like every desperate alcoholic — with limited and faulty understandings. But begin we must, to search for the One we have so little knowledge about, who exists on the other side of so many barriers that block our way. Possibly the only truth that we can embrace with any degree of confidence is that HE IS (I AM is his name – see below). Possibly the only "proof" we have that this fact has any merit is that we have come to realize that he must exist simply because we need him so! We have come to the understanding that he is our only, our last hope.

When Moses (1400 BCE) encountered God at the burning bush, he too, and the children of Israel with him, faced an impossible situation. The people, enslaved for 400 years, and Moses exiled to the backside of the desert, all did seem beyond hope. Into this impossible situation God revealed himself by his name, simply "I AM" or even more enigmatic "I Am Who I Am" (Exodus 3:14). In short, God is saying, "At this point in your life, I am an undefined *Reality*." As Moses and the children of Israel began their journey with God, they had very, very limited knowledge of this God. They most certainly had a lot of wrong notions, having lived in a pagan setting for 400 years. Interestingly God gave them no theology lesson, simply "I AM" (YHWH, or with vowels added Yahweh). By implication, no more than simply, "Trust me, I am *Real!*"

The Exodus story continues. As they journeyed along, God repeatedly added the predicate, the verb to this incomplete "I AM" statement. God, slowly over time, bit by bit, revealed himself to the children of Israel **through his interactions with them**. The Old Testament is full of stories of encounters with God, and in these contexts new names, new information is revealed as to who this mystery God is. Here is a list of some of these encounters and the resultant new names for God in the Old Testament. Each of these new names represented more experiential heart-knowing of him.

> Yahweh-jireh = "I AM will provide." (Genesis 22:11-14)
> Yahweh-rapha = "I AM who heals." (Exodus 15:26)
> Yahweh–nissi = "I AM - my banner" after winning a battle.
> (Exodus 17:16)
> Yahweh-mekoddishkem = "I AM who sanctifies you."
> (Exodus 31:12)
> Yahweh-shalom = "I AM your peace." (Judges 6:22-24)
> Yahweh-sabaoth = "I AM God of Hosts" God Almighty.
> (Psalms 22:10)
> Yahweh-raah = "I AM your Shepherd." (Psalms 23:1)
> Yahweh-tsidkenu = "I AM your Saving Justice." (Jeremiah 23:5-6)

Jesus, claiming to be God in human form, continued this tradition of adding more and more meaning to the "I AM" name for God. Again all of these self revelations are in the context of experiences, of God encounters, all as people walked the journey of life.

I AM the Bread of Life. (John 6:48-51)
I AM the Light of the World. (John 8:12)
I AM the Gate for the Sheep. (John 10:7-9)
I AM the Good Shepherd. (John 10:14-16)
I AM the Resurrection and the Life. (John 11:25-26)
I AM the Way, the Truth, and the Life. (John 14:6)
I AM the True Vine. (John 15:5)

The truth we need to embrace as we begin our spiritual quest is that God will progressively make himself known as we journey seeking him. Yes we will need to be willing to let go of our preconceptions, our misconceptions, our tendency to define him on our own terms. If not, we will experience major faith crisis every time he fails to live up to our expectations, i.e. our erroneous concepts as to how he should act in our given life predicaments.

To illustrate the dynamics of the I AM name: when gospel-truth becomes alive in us, then Jesus has become for us "I AM the light of the world". When the burden of guilt is lifted, then God has become for us "Yahweh our Saving Justice". When he helps us gain victories in our struggle with sin, then he has become for us "Yahweh my banner". (The banner symbolizes the flag that is waved when victory is achieved.) When we experience life-giving inner peace he has become for us "I AM the Good Shepherd" or "Yahweh-Shalom, Yahweh our Peace". As we journey on, more and more insights will be given.

The secret of any spiritual quest is simply to get up after every stumble, simply to continue walking, trusting "I AM" to meet us on the way as his love, faithfulness, his wisdom see fit. In humility, we need to be open to have him reveal, i.e. define, or redefine himself to us as individuals and as communities of believers. Over time we will get to know him more correctly.

More comforting still, each of the names listed previously is not only a self revelation of God; each is a promise for us as well. God will be true to his many names in our own spiritual quest as well. Slowly over time, more and more of the Mystery will be lifted, and he will become for us our Abba Father, our Everything!

"God is not a blurry Power living somewhere in the sky, not an abstraction like the Greeks proposed, not a sensual superhuman like the Romans worshiped, and definitely not the absentee Watchmaker of the Deists. God is personal." Philip Yancey, "*The Bible Jesus Read*," *Christianity Today*, January 11, 1999, page 68.

Wrapping our Minds around the Concept of God

Many struggle with the whole idea of God: a spirit, invisible, omnipresent, omniscient, omnipotent (everywhere present, all knowing, all powerful respectively). How could such a God even exist and if he does, possibly take a personal caring interest in me, one of seven billion, so lost in my own troubles and cares?

The Bible uses many metaphors; each showing one characteristic of God: King of Kings, Lord of Lords, Almighty, Ancient of Days, Heavenly Father, Judge, and many more. None is a complete picture. The second of the Ten Commandments warns against making any image of him, presumably because no image can possibly capture all the aspects of God, and being incomplete, any image is inevitably heretical and dangerous.

The Renaissance painters covered the ceilings of chapels depicting God as a human male, larger than life, white haired, with a penetrating gaze, a pointing finger. Have these many pictures fueled our cultural concept of God as a grand grandfather figure in the sky? For many, this "Father image" has become so tainted with the blemishes that we so often associate with the brokenness of fatherhood that permeates our human story. How can we possibly even begin to relate to such a deity!

Possibly these paintings, and the resulting faulty images we carry in our minds (in contravention of the second of the Ten Commandments) need to be exorcised from our minds.

Does God's creation contain better illustrations that could help us move towards a better understanding of God? To be sure, God can never be equated with his creation. He is outside of the cosmos but there are created realities that point towards a better understanding.

- God is the light pushing back the darkness (1 John 1:5).
- He is like the laws of nature, maintaining order, keeping chaos at bay.
- He is like the life principle that enlivens all that lives, keeping death away.
- He is like the air all around and within, every breath sustains.
- He is like the energy inspiring spring, bringing new life, rich joy and so much promise.

And more subtly because of the brokenness within the human family:

- He is the spirit of the Good that does not give up on the human family. History is a record of one era following another where evil threatens to overwhelm the human story but somehow there always come seasons of renewal where the Good does return.
- He is the spirit of Love that inspires every human who chooses to embrace rather than destroy. This love is observed, on the one hand, in a mother's love for her newborn child, and on the other, in the victim who chooses to forgive (1 John 4:8).

All of these realities are invisible, even the light. We only see what it illuminates. All are everywhere present, all seem so all powerful, yet no one thing or person on the planet is so hidden as to be beyond their influence. These are helpful creation illustrations that show how God can be spirit, invisible, everywhere, all knowing, and all powerful yet touch me personally no matter where I may be hiding.

As for God's relational perfection: his compassion, faithfulness, and love, we need only contemplate the gospel stories of Jesus as he tenderly touched individuals no matter how broken or marginalized. (Luke 15 would be a good place to begin.) He took a compassionate interest in every person who turned his way. That has been the testimony of count-less millions through the ages. And it is still true today.

Twelve Steps: The Parameters for a Spiritual Quest

What personal preparations are needed for a successful spiritual quest? What inner attitudes need to be cultivated so as to increase the possibilities of arriving at the destiny – a life transformed, renewed?

We need to be completely committed. If our quest is just an add-on to our busy lives then it will never meet the expectations we have for it. All of these practices, or disciplines as they are called here, need to be birthed from within a deep awareness that our lives are so much more than a coming and going on a physical and social level. The conviction that our lives are foundationally dependent on the vertical dimension must ever grow in depth. Our spirit, not our body, is most important.

There may be times of dedicated focus on these disciplines but ultimately these disciplines need to become the default setting (habits) of our lives as we engage in the necessary activities of living. These disciplines need to create the white space, the margins of our lives, those activities that we naturally slip into when we have some downtime, when we need refreshing, when we find ourselves waiting in a line or possibly driving, or during the long sleepless nights.

Richard Foster, in his popular book *Celebration of Discipline* (see reading list) suggests twelve classic disciplines for birthing and enhancing the spiritual dimension of our lives. These disciplines have been distilled from the long rich history of the Christian tradition.

In our day of instant fast foods, instant lottery success, instant happiness with just that purchase, and instant speed dates we balk at the idea of discipline: hard work, long term commitment to a worthy goal. We need only to observe any athlete who has achieved lofty goals to realize how much this "instant everything" myth misses the mark of reality.

The success of any spiritual quest may be determined by the degree to which we incorporate these disciplines into our journey towards renewal, and conversely, the degree to which we debunk the contradictory myths that we have absorbed from culture.

The purpose of the following section is to provide a short overview of these disciplines. Hopefully this wets the appetite for a life with greater depth, and in the process, charts a pathway that leads to enhancement in the SPIRIT column.

A quick read-through to begin with is encouraged, but eventually the goal would be to spend a week or two with each to "practice" that step. Richard Foster's book *Celebration of Discipline* is recommended for regular reading. This book should be a keeper for every believer's devotional book shelf.

INWARD DISCIPLINES
Pressing into His Presence.

1) Meditation – The goal is to move us into God's healing presence and to bring him into every detail of our lives. God is no longer just a theology, but a living presence, near and transforming. Bible truths are no longer just intellectual concepts but internalized where they can shape life.

Meditation counters the myth that education's primary focus is just the filling of the mind. Education is first of all the shaping of the heart out of which flow the values and the behaviours that shape our lives and destinies.

Meditation firmly underlines the understanding that the Bible is so much more than simply literature. It is the primary bridge to the One who is ever seeking to connect with us. The Author, even more so than the message, is the secret to a life transformed.

Lectio divina (literally sacred reading) is an interactive approach to the Bible that has been developed over the centuries. Some have broken this process down into 4 simple steps.

- **Read**: Focus on a short passage of scripture, from a phrase to a story. Seek to understand the passage in context. A commentary or a Bible handbook may be helpful.
- **Think**: Place yourself in the story, under the truth. Seek to discern any relevance to you and your situations.
- **Pray**: Ask God, "Is there anything you are seeking to tell me through this passage?"
- **Act**: Take any action steps suggested. A word obeyed is a word embraced and becomes a word that shapes.

https://wau.org/archives/article/read_think_pray_act/

Read, Think, Pray, Act "Lectio Divina" in Four Easy Steps, James Martin, SJ

2) **Prayer** – Prayer is possibly more a listening than a talking, more a waiting in God's presence than a wish list.

- Prayer is first of all discerning what God's will is and then believing that God longs to make it so. (E.g. God desires me, and those around me, to become more loving, more holy people. My prayers need to increasingly line up with God's dreams for us.)
- Prayer is becoming partners with God for the changes we sense he wills. Prayer is the bringing of heaven's resources into the brokenness of our hurting human family; the breaking of spiritual strongholds, the opening of channels for mercy and grace, the speaking of blessings.
- Prayer is the spiritual work that undergirds all activity for any degree of long term effectiveness.
- Prayer will only become an integral part of our lives as we cultivate the realization that we are a people with existential needs, a people falling short of the potential of our lives. In response, we

develop the awareness that the spiritual dimension of our lives desperately needs infusions of grace from a source greater than any available to us on earth.

Prayer counteracts the modern myths that we are, with a whole lot of effort on our part, complete and sufficient within ourselves; or that our world is a closed system where chemistry and fate rule. The act of prayer affirms the truth that God can and does make the deciding difference as we bring our lives and longings into alignment with his will.

Prayer is letting go, finding rest, affirming that God is good.

"Our Father in heaven, hallowed be your name,
Your Kingdom come, your will be done
On earth (i.e. in my life, in my sphere of influence)
As it is in heaven." Matt 6:9 ff

3) Fasting – One of the myths of our consumer society suggests that more stuff, more food, more fun, will satisfy the emptiness in our hearts. To fast, to say no to the demands from the body, is a profound way of emphasizing that we have come to recognize that it is the spirit dimension that is critical for wholeness. To calm the appetites of the body is to elevate the sensitivities of the spirit. A day without food, without entertainment, or without digital connections may be a day well spent developing deeper awareness of the more important. Such a day would expose the degree to which we are addicted to the excesses of our culture. Fasting and reflecting will expose the degree to which our self has become controlled by so much that has so little value. So much may even have destructive influence.

The life-giving practices of the spiritual dimension need to be deliberately incorporated into our regular daily routines. To fast is to consciously work towards better *Default* settings.

OUTWARD DISCIPLINES
Seeking Better Alignment with Our Surroundings

4) Simplicity – The three-column exercise (BODY, SOUL, and SPIRIT) in a previous section may have helped us become more aware of the excesses within our culture. These excesses, especially from the BODY column, deaden all spiritual sensitivities. Our addictions to our excesses, or the demands placed on us by the busyness of our lives, may have brought us to the place where we realize that our stuff, our activities, our careers own us rather than we own them. All of our excess may have complicated our lives immensely; maybe our lives have, to a degree at least, become unmanageable. Our lives may be drawn in many different directions, so much so that we feel torn inside. We may have lost our core, our center. In eastern religions, the root cause of all struggles, of all evil, is our attachment to this world. This may very well be an extreme but have we in the West made our home at the other extreme?

It may be a good exercise, a life empowering step, to begin the process of eliminating some of the unnecessary distractions of life; both stuff as well as activity.

Less may prove to be more, much more!

5) Study – Instinct shapes the behaviours of all within the animal world. In a similar way far too many people, far too often, blindly follow the dictates of popular culture (i.e. everyone is doing it) or the popular patterns of our subcultures be it family or church (i.e. we have always done it this way). The discipline of study is the deliberate act of stepping back to analyze and critique, and if necessary reshape the patterns and rhythms of our lives and communities. Effective study will result in new habits, more wholesome living.

- We engage in this discipline by talking less and listening, observing, and reflecting more.

- We engage in this discipline by reading those who have thought deeply about the issues that are being raised by our observations. Many classics (books that have survived the passage of time) are available.
- We engage in this discipline by regularly sitting down with others who, like us, value more thoughtful living, less frivolous talk, more focused discussion that spawn new insights and add mutual encouragement towards life change.

The discipline of study prevents us from having minds that think not, "ears that hear not, eyes that see not" (Ezekiel 12:2, Jeremiah 5:21). Through the humble exercise of this discipline we will be able to uncover the many myths of our culture and subculture that we have unknowingly embraced.

6) Solitude, Silence – Our culture loves noise. Our culture promotes crowds, pushes 24/7 entertainment, thrives on distractions. Our culture has invented umpteen different ways of staying connected. All-pervasive advertising encourages every imaginable craving. Our minds and senses are in over-drive.

Is it time for a reality check? We know that the quiet rhythms of nature refresh. Our hearts are able to rewind when we are able to simply stare into the flicker of a burning campfire or the ebb and flow of waves on the seashore. We long for the companionship of friends where words are no longer necessary. We are renewed in the silence of dreamless sleep.

Martin Laird (see reading list) suggests three doorways to bringing God into our every situation; three steps that help develop a calmed silent mind as a life-giving process. Three doorways, easy to describe on paper, but that need a lifetime to walk through, to master.

- To begin with, when life draining temptation, distraction or mental detour enters our mind we greet it with a prayer rather than a commentary. Instead of allowing that thought to become a story that leads to a full blown anxiety attack or lust, or anger etc.

we greet it with a simple prayer. A prayer like "Father, have mercy" or "Abba Father" or simply "Jesus".

- Second, we quietly identify the sin that lurks within that thought that threatens to disturb our calm: worry, lack of trust, lust, anger, fear, envy, jealousy, hate, etc. This step increases awareness of our destructive thought patterns and becomes a simple confession before God. Instead of becoming a victim of the mind-games that destroy we become a witness to them.
- Third, we recognize that these thoughts, no matter where they come from, have as an agenda to increase separation between God and ourselves, between the source of shalom (peace, wholeness) and our inner being. Instead of pandering to these thoughts by allowing them to become commentary we look "over their shoulders" seeking to connect with the God in whose presence we live. We seek to listen for his whisperings, wait for the flowing of his grace. The goal is to allow more of his life to grow within ours.

The net result is that the thoughts that so often lead to so much turmoil within and so often to destructive actions in our day to day, now become opportunities for a closer walk with Abba Father.

"Be still and know that I am God." Psalm 46:10

7) Submission – Pride (inflated self) is humanity's greatest roadblock to emotional, relational and spiritual health. (There is though, healthy pride in a job well done.) The focus in our discussion is the pride that causes us to place ourselves over and above others, even over God, so as to gain advantage from them.

Self-infatuated pride prevents us from seeing value in other people other than simply as objects for our self-gratification. Pride prevents us from valuing others as persons, from recognizing their contributions. In a similar way, pride prevents us from submitting our agenda to God's agenda. God simply becomes the one we go to, to have him bless *our* plans.

Pride leads to self destruction; we are unable to hear the many corrective messages from others, voices that expose our own blind spots, our
errors and excesses. Pride destroys our relationships; we are rendered
unable to really listen to and empathize with our fellow human beings.

Pride elevates me, diminishes others. Submission values others and
places me into proper relationship with them.

We consciously cultivate submission by learning to listen to not only
the words that others speak, but also their unspoken needs and longings.
We grow in this community building character quality by consciously
honouring the dignity of those with whom we cross paths. Practically,
this will look like acts of self-denial, acts that deliberately seek the wellbeing of others. Over time this will help us develop the ability to listen to
and feel the pain within our communities.

Submission is "ducking low enough so God can touch your husband."
Author: Lysa TerKeurst (and in our context we should change husband
to spouse and add your neighbour, your friend, your enemy.)

8) Service – Today's myth of me-ism, "It's all about me, myself, and I.
I deserve this or that. I have earned such and such", continues to shape
us unless challenged by a radical re-orientation. Concerns for personal happiness and gain, for recognition, become life's most pressing
priorities. Most realize they will never be top dog. All dread becoming
the underdog.

The heart of the servant has come to recognize that all of the above
are desperate measures in a wrong dimension (establishing vertical
pecking order). The servant heart is not the reverse of the struggle for
the top; it is not the race to the bottom.

The servant has awakened to the truth that the healing of the wounded
inward-looking self happens only when it turns outward, to others. The
person who has learned to acknowledge, value, even love others, discov-
ers often quite by accident, the healing of the hurting self. Developing a
lifestyle of daily habits (whether small or large) of doing good to others,
without thought of recognition or reciprocation, enlarges our own souls,

heals our marriages and families, and transforms our communities. A culture of serving one another places our communities firmly into God's sphere of abundant grace.

"It is better to serve than to be served." Matthew 20:28

9) Confession – Confession challenges the myth that my sins are someone else's fault: bad parenting, bad church, bad friends, economic disadvantage or lack of opportunity. Confession challenges the myth that "It's not really that bad and besides, everyone else is doing it". As I confess, I personally take ownership of my sins, no ifs or buts. As I confess, I acknowledge that my sin is ultimately rebellion against God's divine order.

But as I confess my sins to my Creator, I affirm that in some eternally mysterious way a Holy God is able to completely forgive me because of the cross of Jesus Christ. As I confess I acknowledge that a restored relationship with Deity is able to sustain me as I learn to live as Jesus would have me live.

In many church circles confession has become a wholly private affair, just between God and self. In Catholic circles with the more public confessional booth, confessing to a priest remains the norm. Confession must involve both. Confessing to a mature believer, who is able to audibly speak God's forgiveness to me, must again find a place in our practice (John 20:23, James 5:16). We are, after all a priesthood of believers (1 Peter 2:5). Secrets have a devastating hold on our lives and have destroyed many. Confessing my sins to the God of all grace in the presence of a mature believer short circuits the strangle hold of secret sins. The church first needs to be a fellowship of sinners before it can mature into a fellowship of saints (Foster, *Celebration of Discipline*, 145).

"God meets the human condition where it
stands most in need, in its poverty
and brokenness." (Laird, reading list)

COMMUNITY DISCIPLINES
Strengthening the Heart's Centre

10) Worship – Worship is foundationally about experiencing a paradigm shift at the core of our being. We begin and move through life believing that everything revolves around us. Our culture seeks, through advertising, to keep this myth alive.

- Worship is born when we begin to realize that our lives revolve around God. The BODY, SOUL, SPIRIT exercise in a previous section hopefully birthed the truth that the spiritual dimension is most important. Worship begins with the awareness that the spiritual dimension, our relationship with God, is foundational.

Nature illustrates this paradigm shift. We begin our lives observing the sun revolving around our planet. With study we discover that our planet and all the life it supports is absolutely dependent on the sun. Our dependence on the sun, not just for spring and harvest but for the very birth of the planet, for stability within the expanse of space, for the security of the rhythms, and the energy that make life possible, becomes overwhelming. If it were not for the revelation that the Creator God is the ultimate source of it all, it would be perfectly understandable if we all would be devoted worshippers of the sun.

- The initial worship response is simply learning to give thanks for all the good things we enjoy. Everything on the planet traces its ultimate source back to the sun. All good things in our lives, similarly trace their ultimate source back to God.
- The worship response grows when we begin to realize that all these good gifts are ours to enjoy only as long as, and to the degree that, we live in harmony with God. With respect to our existence as a planet in space, there is no future in developing our own independent orbit. The planet will do infinitely better when it moves in harmony with the rhythms created by the sun.

In the same manner, the worship response of reverential fear would have us order our lives to the will of God on whose blessing we are so completely dependent. Worship will inevitably lead to transformation of our lives. To worship is to change. The change itself is worship.

- Our worship response overwhelms when we realize that God does not meet us like the cold laws of physics (as the sun does the earth) but like the Father does the prodigal son (Luke 15:11). He is passionately waiting for a repentant heart response from us, before rushing out to meet and embrace us.
- The worship response becomes our life when we realize that our heavenly Father has, with tremendous cost to himself, reopened the way for a full return into the life-giving orbit of his divine love.

This growing worship response is expressed through the many liturgies and forms present within the church. The key however must always be his Spirit touching, enlivening our spirit. Without this Spirit-spirit fellowship all may be nothing more than empty form.

True worship transforms the worshiper into that which is worshiped.

11) Guidance – The spiritual journey is in one sense very personal; heart truths can only be discovered individually. Having admitted to this, it is still very helpful, even essential, to have a guide, a mentor who is travelling this journey many paces ahead of us. Some Christian traditions still encourage the office of spiritual director, the go-to-guide for in-depth discipleship for newer believers.

- The encouraging word, the testimony of blessings received, the counsel along the way may be just what is needed to keep an individual moving forward.
- The mentor can hold us accountable, and challenge us to keep pressing on. Breakthroughs are "given" to those who continue past the points of seeming failure, the seeming "all is lost" stage.

- In this partnership, the mentor can help us cultivate the deep expectation (faith) that we are not just moving forward into the great unknown, we are moving towards Someone who is coming to meet us along the way! (In a very real sense that Someone may already be meeting us through the person of the mentor.)

The cultural myth of our fierce individualism prevents us from becoming bonded to the spiritual family with whom we pilgrim. The journey was never meant to be travelled alone. Another cultural myth that stands in our way of the full benefiting of a mentor is the cultural lie that older people have nothing more to offer the younger, "technologically-more-with-it," the "youth-is-where-it's-at," generation. A willingness to sit at the feet of the older generation is a lost art that needs to be re-awakened.

> The tech revolution, enhanced digital connectivity has, at best, minimal impact on the spiritual journey we all must take. We all need to discover "life" the very same way our ancestors did, hence the value of a spiritually mature mentor.

12) Celebration – It has the ring of a command, "Rejoice in the Lord always. I will say it again, rejoice!" (Phil 4:19). It is an observation of reality, the way we as creatures, as human beings function best. Joy is like sunshine, it enlivens, but sadness clouds our days. The church has often been guilty of encouraging an otherworldly, a this-world-denying, version of spirituality. Christianity's early immersion in Greek Platonic thinking caused it to absorb too much of a negative view of the things of this world. Feasting and celebrating were very much a part of Hebraic culture, Christianity's deeper roots; seven annual feasts were mandated within Jewish culture. Celebration is also built into creation. On the one hand, we can look at the many joy-inspiring dimensions of creation around us. On the other, we need to look at our bodies (e.g. the traditional five senses and so many more: sense of beauty and humor, of empathy and appreciation of companionship, awareness of physical, emotional, and spiritual wellbeing) that God gave us with which to enjoy life. There is good reason to believe that God intended that celebration be at the core of our existence.

When the above disciplines are correctly understood and practiced then celebration will be restored to a more central place in our walk with God and with each other. The goal of the disciplines is after all to bring healing and wholeness into our psyche, into our relationships and communities. The disciplines fine-tune our senses so as to again take in more of the beauty and goodness all around. To allow God to come back into our lives is to receive life, and in abundance (John 10:10). Christians have many occasions to celebrate and to overflow with thankfulness. It is indeed a sin not to, when there are so many reasons to!

"The joy of the Lord is our strength." Nehemiah 8:10

This brief introduction to these twelve disciplines was placed here with the goal of wetting our appetites for more wholesome living and to chart a pathway for the spiritual journey that leads to life more abundant.

These twelve disciplines need to be revisited regularly as we journey through life. They will over time become the default patterns of our lives. With every pass, every visit, we develop a deeper tap root into the spiritual fountain of life.

Judeo-Christian spirituality is not a striving
to experience God in his domain
but a working towards bringing God into our everyday.
The Psalms and the Sermon on the Mount
are examples of this down-to-earth spirituality.

"Consciously develop a heart-set of worship, submission, listening to Jesus – allow this to undergird all of life's activities." Thomas Kelly

A promise that encourages …
This is what the high and lofty One says, he who lives forever, whose name is Holy, "I live in a high and lofty place, but also with him who is contrite and lowly in spirit (deep personal awareness of brokenness and incompleteness) to revive the spirit of the lowly and to revive the heart of the contrite." Isaiah 57:15.

PATHWAY TO CONFIDENCE

1. Empowering Spirituality

2. *Cultural Awareness*

3. Religious Literacy

4. Validating our Faith Assumptions

5. Encountering the Kingdom Story

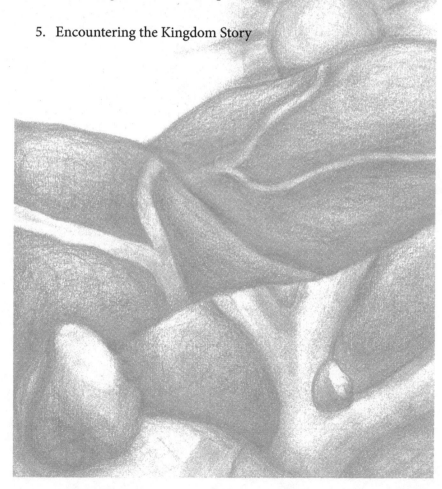

Part 2: Cultural Awareness

a few thoughts to begin with...

The previous section was an invitation to pursue the spiritual dimension of our humanity. Throughout history many have taken up that challenge by first of all retreating from mainstream culture into isolated likeminded communities. The belief was that the surrounding culture presented too many temptations, distractions, and too many contrary headwinds. It was best to live separated from culture.

Such a retreating may not be an option for most of us. History has shown that such isolation does not necessarily promote long term

Some examples are early Christianity's hermit culture and medieval monasticism. After the Reformation, we see the Hutterite and Amish communities retreating from culture.

spiritual health. Most of us are pursuing spirituality under the principle, "In the world but not of the world" (John 17:15-17).

As we seek to grow spiritually in the context of our families, our communities, our culture we will invariably encounter strong headwinds.

This next section presents some of the cultural headwinds that we will inevitably encounter. If we are not aware of them they could trip us up. How many young travellers have left the faith simply because they failed to negotiate these storms? For some, these cultural challenges have become detours, for others stumbling blocks, for yet others, dead-ends.

Those who have taken the time to understand the cultural roadblocks may find faith strengthened when they do encounter them.

Confronting a Cultural Taboo – "Religion"

The word "religion" has fallen on hard times. In popular culture today religion is seen to be the cause of so much conflict, and to boot, so much backwardness. This public rejection of the word and the topic has created an informational vacuum within culture and within all of our personal lives. This has generated its own set of problems. Many have rejected spirituality because it has become tainted by its association with religion.

In Victorian England (19th century), "sex" was a word that had fallen on hard times. A cultural unwillingness to talk about it was so strong that "Victorian England" is known for its prudishness with respect to sex. It does not take much imagination to realize that this lack of appropriate discussion around the topic must have created many personal disasters with respect to relationships and sexuality. How many young lives must have been destroyed before they had even really started because of this lack of information! How much potential for personal joy and fulfillment must have been short-changed! Thankfully our culture has corrected this problem, possibly to the other extreme, but that is another topic for another day.

It is our contention that every person is religious at their very core. (Before you slam this book shut please allow me to explain.)

- Everyone has a set of Life's Ultimate Questions.
- Everyone has answers to these questions. Many may never have thought much about them but if pressed or during crisis situations these answers do surface. For some the answers may be tentative, hesitant, and that may be unsettling. (It may be time to work on them!)
- Everyone's answers are saturated with assumptions that cannot be proved, that have to be accepted by faith (even the atheist's).

All of the above are the domain of religion. Therefore, it is safe to assume that everyone is religious at their very core. How each one practices their "religion" would make for interesting discussion. (This brief description as to what religion really is will be dealt with more fully in the next section.)

To avoid the topic of religion is to deny the core of our humanity and the mystery that embraces our short journey across life's stage. The unwillingness to discuss the topics that religion raises may be creating the informational vacuum that is at the root of so many of the volatile problems within our lives personally, as well as in our global community.

Religion is critical to our lives. When disaster strikes it is all too obvious that those affected usually turn to traditional religion. (The funerals inevitably happen in temples and churches.) Only religion seems to have the resources to help people begin to cope with pain and suffering and the seeming meaninglessness of it all. Invariably it is religion (reviewing and reaffirming our foundational assumptions) that helps us put our lives back together again. It is religion that gives us the strength to pick up the pieces and continue on.

Not just disasters and life's many challenges, but the everyday needs religion as well. It is through religion that we discover meaning for our lives. Who am I, why am I here, what makes life worth living, and what gives me a reason big enough to put up with all the nonsense of our chaotic existence?

It is through religion that we learn to live together in community. It is religion that provides the basis for treating each other with respect and dignity. Ethics, our convictions with respect to right and wrong, is rooted in religion. Our search for ultimate truths is guided by the foundational assumptions that are the essence of religion.

To be sure, religion does complicate our lives immensely. Big issues are complex; that should be expected! It raises ultimate questions that scream for answers during the many crises of our lives. It does raise issues, which if not answered, debilitate us completely. For some the solution is to find an exit to life itself. For others it is an attitude of "eat drink and be merry for tomorrow we die". Maturity would recommend a careful, thoughtful search of this ultimate frontier of human discovery. Only such a religious (spiritual) quest does justice to the mystery of our humanity.

The popular charge that religion is an evil that needs to be eradicated for the wellbeing of humanity needs to be answered. To be sure religion has been at the center of so much evil throughout world history. But so have economic resources, so have ideologies like communism and fascism, so has sex (the Trojan wars were fought over the divinely beautiful Helena) so has the ethics of revenge, so has alcohol, and we could go on and on. The common factor in all of these issues is the human heart and its desperate and so often pathological self-centeredness. Religion is the domain that asks, "Why?" Whenever psychology, criminology or sociology (or any other 'ology' for that matter) addresses these issues they are religious by nature, i.e., they are ultimately operating on the basis of foundational religious assumptions: what does it mean to be human, what does it mean to be good, and what is with all the bad in us?

Atheism's visceral anger came out of the closet after the 9/11 attacks on the Twin Towers in New York City. This anti-any-religion reaction is further strengthened every time the media picks up a story of a religious extremist on a rampage of some sort. Actions by extremists, fundamentalists, religious fanatics etc. all make terrific nation-wide headlines (by our left-leaning media) so often far beyond the scope of the actual event.

We do need to remember, however, that many horrific events are perpetrated by seemingly "non religious" people (e.g. mass shootings more than once a day within the USA). Possibly many of these random acts of violence are committed by people who have absorbed the religion (or unreligion) of modernism (i.e. there is no god, no judgment day, no karma, I am just an evolved animal with natural inborn aggression, this is how I create my meaning in this senseless existence, death is the end, go out with a bang, etc.)

This visceral reaction against religion may seem logical from within our contemporary western mindset but it may be very misguided.

Atheists are asking the question, "Is religion at the root of so much evil?" That may be the wrong question to ask. We should be asking:

- What is it about religion that can cause it to be such a powerful force for so much evil ... as well as so much good? (For Christianity think anti - slavery, beginnings of public education, hospitals, democracy, care of poor, etc.)

The answer is not to avoid the topic of religion as our culture is hellbent on doing. The much better answer is to create the forum that allows for personal reflection, for honest and respectful discussion, for debate and for research surrounding the issues raised.

My hope is that this book is a help, a guide for this quest that must be taken if our individual lives are to develop the heart-center that enables us to live with meaning and purpose. This personal quest is the ultimate coming of age story of our lives. It sets the parameters for a life that hopes to be well lived.

The ultimate challenge we all face is to understand the mystery of our lives. Religion is one of the pieces of that puzzle. It may very well be the most important piece, the piece that integrates all the rest. To question that statement may mean that we are unaware as to what religion really is.

Religion is Best Understood as a Cosmic Story

What are some popular understandings of what religion is?

- Some define religion as God-talk and as church and temple visits.
- Some define religion as the public expression of private spirituality.
- Many experience religion as ancient inherited traditions.
- Some see religion as a set of archaic teachings set in stone.
- Many view it as a set of values; life principles that define good behaviours.
- Some view religion even more superficially, a list of do's and don'ts, a set of rules that in today's context seem to make no sense.
- Others see religion as a searching for esoteric (otherworldly) experiences.

All of these perspectives are just a part of the picture, essentially only the tip of the iceberg. To judge a religion based on such limited understandings does not do justice to its essence. To reject a parent's religion on the basis of such a shallow perspective may possibly be a life-destroying mistake.

The heart of any religion is the cosmic story that undergirds it (described a bit later). Without that cosmic story the above list will all fall away, often as so much unnecessary and outdated baggage for our journey through life.

This is really not a redefinition of religion. Religion has always been faith in a cosmic story. It is just that for most, God is the primary and overpowering character in the story. It is God who overwhelmingly shapes and defines the story. As a result, when someone thinks "religion" the word "God" usually comes to mind first. And conversely, even for the atheist, it is God's absence that defines atheism's cosmic story much like the wintry North Pole is defined by the absence of the sun.

Evangelical Christians love to say, "Christianity is not a religion, it is a relationship (with God)." This, it seems to me, is something that we should stop saying. This, God-relationship-talk, still keeps the focus on religion as God-talk. This falls nicely into the lap of Atheists who continue to say, "We can't possibly be a religion, because we have "discovered" that there is no one out there."

> The term 'religion' may need a renaissance in our day. How can we possibly begin to address the deep roots of the issues that plaque our modern cultures if we are loathe to even name the term that refers to those roots.

By stressing the correct understanding of religion as cosmic story, we reinforce the fact that atheism is a religion as well, because it too, has a cosmic story.

What gives religion its power for good as well as for evil? Definitely not its trappings: traditions, lists of do's and don'ts, teachings, etc. It is the cosmic story underneath these religious trappings that takes hold of the human heart and imagination. It is the cosmic story that inspires humans to act so powerfully, either for good or ill.

What enables a sub-culture, or a family, to successfully pass their religion on to the next generation? Again it is the cosmic story that must captivate the mind and heart of its youth. If all that youth receive are the traditions, the do's and don'ts, then these will inevitably fall by the wayside as so much outdated baggage. Our young people will unknowingly absorb the prevailing cultural story subconsciously and this contradictory cosmic story will provide new traditions and behaviours, most likely very much at odds with their parents' perspectives.

A people group whose cosmic story has been destroyed suffers loss of identity; life loses meaning. The people group loses the inner strength to carry on. Is this the cause of so much suffering within our neighbours, the First Nations people? Forced assimilation, loss of language and loss of their cultural celebrations have resulted in the loss of much of their cosmic story.

Conversely, a people group whose story refuses to die, cannot cease to exist. Is this the reason why the Jewish people have overcome the greatest of existential threats, the greatest of assimilation efforts during their 4000 year struggle for survival? Their cosmic story refuses to die!

Mother story, Cosmic story, Worldview, Meta-story, Meta-narrative. (Meta is a prefix added to words to refer to that which is beyond, above, deeper, more basic etc – "the story that is foundational to all stories.") In this section, as throughout the book, I use these words interchangeably. My language is groping for a strong enough word to describe this biggest of stories.

*** from the beginning to the end of time, with an underlying problem that has consumed us all from the first generation till now, with an undying hope that there might yet be a solution, we are all characters in this biggest of stories, our personal problems are just expressions of this underlying problem, our longings for better things just the eternal bubbling up of this ageless hope ***

What is it about STORY that so powerfully influences our lives, often at levels below conscious awareness? A little detour may be needed to help us reconnect with all the stories that we love and live and struggle with. This detour will provide the context for the cosmic story that forms the subconscious foundational framework for all of our lives.

THE POWER OF STORY

Humankind thrives on stories. Little children can be mesmerized by stories. All cultures shape the next generation through its stories. A good story engages us to a much greater degree than any logical argument. The best speakers are the ones who teach through story. Imagination and not just the mind are stirred. Empathy or euphoria, sadness and despair, deeper longings and sensitivities all can be brought to the surface through the art of good story telling. Stories are put to music, they are dramatized. They are illustrated in many different ways, from paintings to monuments to museums. We are hardwired to respond deeply to story.

We can diagram the typical story in the following way. The basic elements of every story include an over-arching theme, a set of characters, a setting, the plot (the struggle that needs to be overcome), a resolution of the struggle, and the conclusion, (the new normal).

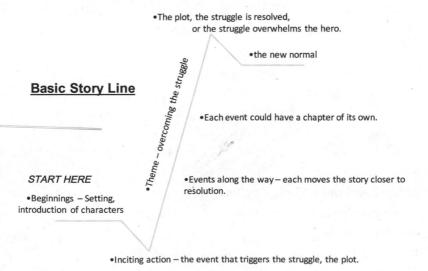

Start Reading at Bottom Left

•The plot, the struggle is resolved,
or the struggle overwhelms the hero.

•the new normal

Basic Story Line

Theme – overcoming the struggle

•Each event could have a chapter of its own.

START HERE

•Beginnings – Setting,
introduction of characters

•Events along the way – each moves the story closer to
resolution.

•Inciting action – the event that triggers the struggle, the plot.

OUR LIVES AS A STORY

Possibly this fascination with story is because each one of us is really living a story. The main events do include birth, youth, maturity, and legacy (death really, but that makes our story a tragedy and in our culture we do not like going there). The story will include struggles and challenges, maybe an all consuming life goal, a theme if you will. We can use the basic story line to illustrate the typical human story as well. We are all very conscious of this story. It includes all the chapters of our lives. Our friends, our significant relationships, our educational endeavors, our career exploits, our adventures, our major struggles in life that we either overcome or that eventually defeat us, all are part of our story. Those who have accomplished great things write autobiographies. Others have biographies written about their lives and achievements. It is interesting that today more and more "ordinary" people are putting their story to paper. Most life stories are really worth telling.

Mark Twain said that each person has two defining days in their life. The day that they were born and secondly the day they begin to realize why. Any story worth telling begins on that day. It is indeed sad, when someone never stops long enough to discover the reason why s/he was born. The result is a shallow story indeed.

AWARENESS OF A LARGER STORY

Every human life will also include a degree of awareness of something much bigger than what is typically recorded in their personal story line. We are deeply aware that life is about so much more than meets the eye.

We all ask questions like, "Where did I come from? What happens to me after I die? and, Is there value to my life?" We all search for meaning in life. We all struggle with the reality of the inevitable negatives that

Life's Ultimate Questions: Exploring the Stories that Shape Our Everyday

seem to come out of nowhere and mess up our journey through life and we ask "Why?" and "Where did that come from?" All of these questions, and the answers we need for them, confirm that we are all part of a much larger story.

LIFE'S DEEPER STORY QUESTIONS

- The Question of Truth – The Foundational Question.
  - What is truth, and how can it be validated?
  - Is there a Higher Power, if so, what are the dynamics of our relationship with 'Him'?

- The Questions Surrounding our Humanity.
  - What does it mean to be human?
  - What is the purpose of our lives?

- The Question of Ethics.
  - What are life-enhancing behaviors?
  - How do we unwrap our sexuality, this greatest of personality gifts, so that it is life-giving rather than life-destroying?

- The Questions Surrounding Evil and Suffering.
  - Where does evil come from?
  - Why is suffering and loss so universal?
  - What is the solution to the seemingly universal human tendency towards evil?

- The Questions Surrounding the Future.
  - What happens to us after death?
  - How does the cosmic story end?
  - What gives us hope sufficient to help us survive in the most challenging of situations?

Every thinking person has these questions and together they imply a much larger story. Therefore, everyone has a larger story than simply the superficial one that starts with birth and ends with death. Even the atheist who believes that death is the end for an individual realizes that there is a larger cosmic story. The human DNA molecule is on the journey towards something beyond today's normal.

It is this larger story that
- gives us the answers to life's deeper questions.
- provides the parameters as to how I interpret all of the events and experiences of my life.
- creates the context and provides the inspiration for our individual personal stories.

In our secular culture, this larger story is generally referred to as our worldview. This cosmic story provides the framework as to how we understand the world and life and all that it embraces, including me and my life story. We consider this cosmic story as factual even though upon examination we can easily recognize that it is riddled with assumptions that we have accepted by faith. This larger story, this worldview, is our religion. Everyone, even the atheist has one. Many have never thought deeply or coherently about their adopted larger story but when probed, the elements of that larger story do reveal themselves.

Each religion, each worldview can be illustrated using the story line diagram as well.

Beginning reading at lower left

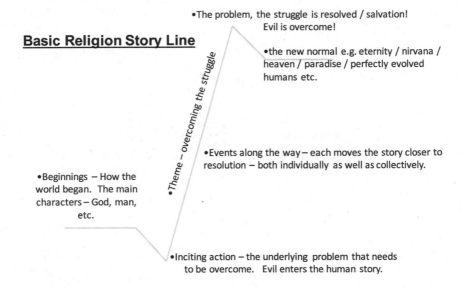

Basic Religion Story Line

•The problem, the struggle is resolved / salvation! Evil is overcome!

•the new normal e.g. eternity / nirvana / heaven / paradise / perfectly evolved humans etc.

Theme – overcoming the struggle

•Events along the way – each moves the story closer to resolution – both individually as well as collectively.

•Beginnings – How the world began. The main characters – God, man, etc.

•Inciting action – the underlying problem that needs to be overcome. Evil enters the human story.

Part 3 presents the cosmic stories of the world's major religions.

Every religion has such a cosmic story line. Every culture has … more than that, is being shaped by such a story line. It is, to a large part, the glue that keeps that culture together. Even an atheistic culture, like modernism or communism, needs one for life's larger context and as the inspiration for its culture shaping agenda.

Every human being has one! This larger story may be unknown and unexamined. It may be eclectic (you have subconsciously picked and chosen elements from various stories and as a result it will have internal contradictions). The individual's larger story line will be aligned with reality, as the majority culture and its foundational story line have defined it, to a lesser or greater degree. These personal and cultural religious story lines are all rooted in deeply held, subconscious assumptions. We absorb these assumptions without our awareness from the culture into which we have been born. It is only later in life that some begin to seriously question these subconscious assumptions. And this questioning generally only happens when confronted with a significant life crisis or by a different story line, a different religion.

It is this cosmic story that provides the foundation to the teachings, the behaviours, and the traditions that have been passed on to us. Without the cosmic story, these superficial trappings may not really make much sense.

Are so many young people today walking away from their parents' religion because they have never really encountered and embraced the cosmic story that undergirds their parents' faith?

Awareness of the cosmic story that we are living will help us understand our own responses to the dilemmas of our lives. Our inability to experience deeper transformation within our lives may be rooted in our inability to change the cosmic story in which we are participating.

Any significant change in our personal lives will only happen if we consciously change the story we are living. The most effective way of making any change more permanent is to change one's community (adopting a community whose cosmic story is more in keeping with the one I am trying to live).

Do We Even Need God?

I wrestled with the following question, with this cultural roadblock, when I needed to walk along Burrard Avenue in Downtown Vancouver.

I had a lot of time on my hands to experience this civic jewel within the province of BC. Amazing buildings, inviting atmosphere, advanced cultural symbols, busy well-dressed professionals, a city that seemed to have arrived in every sense of the word! Why would anyone want to jeopardize this aura of excellence with a crazy question like…

Our school bus had broken down and our week-long Youth with a Mission (YWAM) school trip seemed in disarray! We were in Vancouver to help our grade 11 class develop greater life and God awareness. (This bus problem did become a faith encouraging God-story.)

Do We Even Need God?

Our forefathers had no problem admitting the reality of a power greater than themselves in the universe. First of all, they were pressed by problems that seemed so overwhelming to them. So much of their lives was so utterly influenced by forces they could not control. The seemingly regular occurrences of famine, disease and war were just a few of these situations that helped shape a belief in and encouraged a dependence on a power beyond human-kind. Second, they were surrounded by mysteries that awed or terrified them, mysteries they did not understand.

Today with our knowledge of science and the tremendous progress we have made in understanding our world and in controlling some of its problems, the need for such a higher power often does seem so outdated, so irrelevant and so fictitious. Many have adamantly rejected such a notion and for many more the "higher power" is simply part of a Sunday-only tradition that just lingers on.

How does one respond to such a radical reversal for the various God-camps?

A) Facing Problems and Struggles

For generations past, it was the problems and the challenges of life that encouraged faith in a higher power. We would suggest that today's problems and challenges are as great, if not greater than those of yester year and that today's generation is simply closing its eyes and hearts to this reality. If problems do surface then a blind faith in science alleviates many an existential fear. For many, a confident faith in the power of science to solve not only the problems it has created but the rest of the problems as well, remains unquestioned. Furthermore, a faith in the unseen processes of evolution, whose inevitable force is to move all life-forms ever onward and upward, inspires confidence in the future.

Is such a confident faith in the powers of science, technology, evolution reasonable? Our problems are many but…

Our very real problems are hidden
     behind all the glitter and the glamour of our western mega
          cities, (Burrard Avenue!)
     underneath all the layers of our rationalizations and excuses,
     beyond the reach of our calloused consciences.

We humans ignore or are ignorant of the problems because we are
     distracted by endless and so often mindless
          entertainment possibilities.
     benumbed by myriad addictions both old and new.

befuddled by redefinitions e.g. abortions, gendercide become
prochoice, marriage breakdown becomes alternative
lifestyles, sodomy becomes ???. (How many destructive
issues are hidden under the label of political correctness?)
muzzled to ignore negative messages. The positive thinking
panacea of our culture demands the silencing of any
negative messengers. These "prophets of doom" are often
denounced as cultural misfits.

Our problems continue to be very real. Our contention is that we
have developed a culture that refuses to take them seriously. Even media
news casts of disasters and problematic mega-issues are processed more
as entertainment for consumption rather than as warnings for personal reflection!

Just a short list of some of the mega-issues we are facing:

International problems: exploitation of poor countries,
human slavery (apparently as prolific now as ever), human
trafficking (mostly women and children destined for the
sex trade in our glamorous mega-cities), the degradation
of the environment, destruction of biodiversity (decreased
diversity translates into weakening of life-forms), corrupting power of multinationals over local governments,
climate change, unpredictable extreme weather events,
repeated failures of the UN to solve international crisis,
religious extremism, and so on.

Cultural problems: the growing divide between rich and
poor. Some have earned as much by morning coffee-break
on January 1 (and they may still be in bed!) as most earn
the whole year. Industrial and corporate greed paying lip-
service to local needs and the environment. Food security
(local food independence lost in many areas), reduced food
quality (pesticides, herbicides, preservatives, GMO's etc.),

resource depletion, homelessness, racism, violence, unfathomable national economic debts, and the list goes on.

Personal problems: personal addictions, depression, anger
issues, suicide (highest for young people ever), marriage
and family breakdown, child abuse and neglect, crippling
guilt, loneliness, meaningless of life, loss of hope, chronic
diseases (believed to be a product of our modern way of
life) and more, until we reach the ultimate fear, the fear of
our own demise.

Indeed our problems have not gone away! Many would argue they
have increased; some would suggest that cataclysmic failures are pending
on many fronts. Our culture ignores God, a higher power. One reason
for such a denial is that at a cultural level, we keep pushing our problems
to the back burner. (Possibly we are overwhelmed personally, but culturally it seems to be, "More entertainment talk shows and if some itty-bitty
action does happen, well publicized lip-service!")

We can learn a valuable lesson from the 12 step Alcoholics
Anonymous program. These steps, refined in the crucible of life-threat-
ening pain and personal existential struggle repeatedly affirm the need
to connect with a higher power, with the "God of our understanding".
These steps have given hope and a new lease on life for many.

The first three steps of AA (Alcoholics Anonymous) adapted by many
groups struggling with addictions are that we…

1. Admitted we were powerless over alcohol — that our lives had
   become unmanageable.

2. Came to believe that a power greater than ourselves could restore
   us to sanity.

3. Made a decision to turn our will and our lives over to the care of
   God as we understood him.

Do we need God? Do we need to connect with a higher power? When we honestly consider humanity's problems and our endless attempts to get a handle on them, then we too are encouraged to consider these questions with greater humility and greater longing. *If there is a God, a higher power, then there is hope!*

We need to move beyond ignorance of the problems that are threatening on so many fronts. We can respond by continuing to have a "blind faith in science and evolution" or we can choose a "blind faith in a higher power". The other option is to lose all hope and many have!

B) Living with the Mysteries

The second reason that encouraged our forefathers to pursue a faith in a higher being was the reality of so much that was mysterious in their life experiences. From lightning and thunder, to the birth of a child, life was filled with so much that defied explanation. One needed a God to explain these awe inspiring or terror filled realities. But now humans have cultivated the confidence that science does, or soon will, explain all of these mysteries. The need to have a god for the stuff we do not understand has resulted in a god who continues to lose more and more relevance. The more science unlocks the secrets of the universe and of life itself, the smaller the "God of the Gaps" becomes.

> The gaps in scientific knowledge were, for a time, used to argue for the existence of God. Dietrich Bonheoffer's answer to this faulty theology is helpful.
>
> "How wrong it is to use God as a stop-gap for the incompleteness of our knowledge. If in fact the frontiers of knowledge are being pushed further and further back (and that is bound to be the case), then God is being pushed back with them, and is therefore continually in retreat. We are to find God in what we know, not in what we don't know."
>
> Quoted in Wikipedia, "God of the Gaps"

Science continues to provide sound explanations for more and more of the mysteries that puzzled our forefathers. But the reality is that with every new discovery, deeper layers of mysteries are uncovered. Instead of having the gaps shrink we are experiencing gaps that are growing in depth. The mysteries of our world are becoming more complex, more significant and more perplexing. Science continues to broaden our horizons, but with these expanded horizons more unknowns, more mysteries are continually being brought to the surface.

Second, the fact that science is providing great explanations for the mysteries that puzzled our forefathers does not eliminate the need for God. Just because science has "fully" explained the processes that create the birth of a child, does not mean that God is no longer necessary. Everyone who has experienced the birth a child will stand in awe at what has just occurred. A mystery explained is no less a mystery that amazes. The joy created, the thankfulness that bubbles up, the wonder that awes, the new life that awaits, all suggest a deep need to turn somewhere, to someone to acknowledge the debt, to say thanks, to pay tribute, to worship if you will.

A mystery explained does not necessarily eliminate the need for God. Rather it should move us closer to the God who made it all possible. All the fine-tuned laws of nature that make life in such abundance possible should cause us to stop and stand in awe and wonder. They should cause us to ask even more "Who has made this possible?" rather than simply to conclude, "Oh the majesty of chance!"

The amazing discoveries of science should awaken more awe and wonder rather than less. It is true that our generation has lost so much of this awe and wonder for the mysteries that are being uncovered. May this loss not be partly responsible for the lack of respect that we are showing creation and the environment around us? Is it possible, that by eliminating God from the equation, we have lost the reverence for the "magic" of the world in which we live? Is the lack of awe and wonder causing us humans to do untold damage to our environment? The worship of ourselves, as survivor, as the fittest, as de facto owner because we are the "top dog" in the universe, may be leading to the degradation of the amazing world in which we live.

The healthier response to "the awe and wonder of a world dissected" ought to awaken within us a worship response to the Higher Power that made it all possible. The result may very well be a more wholesome care for creation.

It is true that popular Christendom has been blamed with promoting the raping and pillaging of the environment simply because the focus is on the "New Heaven and the New Earth in the sweet bye and bye". This criticism has merit. Popular Christianity and biblical Christianity may be worlds apart with respect to creation care. As believers in the God who created the world which was declared very good, and a world that will be redeemed, the church must repent and become the people that take great care of the "entrusted to us" world. After all God will "destroy those who destroy the earth" Revelations 11:18.

Atheism is a Religion – Humans are Religious by Nature

The purpose of this section is two fold.

> **First of all we will seek to show that secular atheism, the belief system of our modern western cultures, is indeed a belief system, a religion.** This will be proved using the standard three statement logical **syllogism** of philosophy, classic deductive reasoning.
>
> #1 All religions, and all religious people, have certain characteristics and act in a certain way.
>
> #2 Secular Atheism has these same characteristics and its adherents act in that same way.
>
> #3 Therefore Secular Atheism is a religion.

For too long atheistic secularism has maintained that it alone is neutral, that it alone is not a religion. This, followers maintain, allows them to be a judge of all the others. Their position, they claim, is based on nothing but facts, proven by science. The other religions are all based on assumptions that can't be proved. This claim must be exposed for what it is. It is one of the great myths, one of the great lies of our modern culture.

Many leaders within our cultures, who are personally religious, believe they need to leave their religion at home. They, too, have bought into the myth (at least in practice) that Secular Atheism, Liberal Humanism is neutral. Instead of leaving the field wide open for the atheists they need to engage in much soul searching as to how to best be true to their religious roots without offending in the public marketplace of ideas. Statesmanship, not politics, is needed.

> **Second, we will become aware as to how religion works, how it operates in our lives and how it permeates and shapes all cultures.** Our western cultures are woefully ignorant as to the dynamics of religion. The study of religion has all but been eliminated from curricular studies within our educational institutions.

Is this one of the reasons why America's policies in the Middle East have proven to be so woefully inadequate? Have they failed to incorporate even a basic understanding of Islamic religion into their calculations?

This lack of understanding as to how religion functions is also seen in the inadequacy of many of the social policies of today. Marriages are failing. (Has traditional marriage been devalued by the redefinition of marriage?) Families, the all important incubator for the raising of the next generation, are falling apart. Too many of our young people are struggling with issues of meaningless and purposelessness. The polarization and fragmentation within so many of our western cultures have their roots in religion as well. The lack of understanding as to how religion works within culture and in all of our hearts creates an inadequate response to these very difficult problems.

Too many of our young people, and adults as well, are being converted to secular atheism without being aware that they are changing their religion. They assume they are leaving religion altogether. That is an epic error. They maybe are being brainwashed without being aware.

The evidence that secular atheism is like every other religion is available. We just need to be willing to challenge the lie that has been presented as fact for so long. And when we consider that our whole culture is being reengineered in keeping with atheistic values, this indeed must be seen as an issue of critical importance.

A) Atheism, like every other religion, has a cosmic story

Every classic religion has a coherent story line, one from the beginning of the world to the distant future when "salvation" will have been achieved. (These story lines will be presented in part 3 of this book. Here we simply need to show that secular atheism belongs in that comparative study as well.)

The secular atheist has such a story line as well. It starts with the Big Bang, the beginning of the physical universe. It continues through all the stages of evolutionary development. We have now arrived at the stage where one life species, humankind, has far out developed all other species. Humankind has convincingly become the fittest in the struggle for survival. Humankind, it is believed, is now within reach of the prize, that of controlling the wilderness within (the heart with its passions) and the wilderness around (the environment through technological breakthroughs). That will be salvation achieved! The human DNA molecule, it is believed, is on an amazing evolutionary journey from simplicity to perfection.

The presence of such a larger story makes secularism a religion like any other. It is a religion that preaches that there is no god but …

B) Atheism, like every other religion, has a power greater than humanity

Religion, by popular definition, is a belief in a power greater than our own. (Religion, more correctly understood, is the story created by this power.) This larger power provides the solution, the salvation that we humans so desperately need. To be sure the secular humanist's salvation will not be enjoyed by us individually but the human DNA molecule and its fully evolved future host will be the beneficiary in some distant future time period.

Life, with its embedded evolutionary principle, is the force that inevitably moves the human DNA molecule forward to a better tomorrow. The fact that it is impersonal, non relational, simply means that humanity does not have to answer to it, is not accountable to it. We humans do not give up our autonomy, our, "We are the masters of our own destiny" mind and heart-set. Many indeed would prefer such a stance!

Evolution is the theory that finally allowed so-inclined people to deny the existence of God on the basis of a rational foundation. It provided logical answers to some of the nagging ultimate life questions that prevented atheists from going public. The questions of origins and meaning, as well as death are all "nicely" answered by this simple yet elegant theory.

C) Atheism makes foundational assumptions like every other religion
The foundational teachings of all religions are outside the sphere of reason. These precepts are beyond the realm of our five senses, therefore beyond the boundaries of science. They can be neither proved nor disproved by the use of reason operating through science which is limited to the material world. The claims, "There is a God" and "There is no god" are both trans-rational, beyond reason. Both make a faith assumption about the spiritual realm. The no-god camp's claim that there is no spiritual realm is not a solution, it just adds another assumption to the mix. Both claims are held as heart assumptions. The questions about the existence of God and the presence of a spiritual realm will forever remain within human experience because we are all so deeply aware that our lives seem to be about so much more than meets the eye. Our culture's focus on superficiality and busyness clouds our eyes to that obvious fact.

The answers to life's ultimate questions, listed elsewhere in this book, all logically flow from the "There is a God" or the "There is no god" foundational assumption. Religion and philosophy have been arguing these questions since the beginning of time and will continue to do so until the end of time. All wise men and women, from ancient times and today as well, know that when seeking answers to these ultimate life questions they are indeed searching realities beyond our physical existence and our five senses. We are at best groping in the shadows. We must make foundational assumptions to answer these questions in order to even begin the reasoning process.

Secular atheism assumes that reason and science can uncover the answers to life's ultimate questions. According to atheism, science is the measure of all truth. If science cannot confirm "truth statements" then that "truth statement" is no longer truth, just myth. But this standard for truth is an assumption.

With respect to ethics, it logically follows that there are no moral absolutes, simply because there is no deity beyond ourselves. Standards of behavior and patterns of organizing ourselves into marriages, families, and clans etc. are all evolved structures; none have been prescribed by deity. It is assumed that all are subject to change because there are no absolutes.

> The claim that "science is the measure of all truth" is itself disproved by that very selfsame claim. That claim "science is the measure of all truth" cannot be established by science itself, therefore, according to that principle, it cannot be true!

With respect to meaning of life, it is assumed, on the basis of evolutionary principles we are all accidents on an accidental planet (an assumption as well). These assumptions dictate that there is no inherent meaning, no inherent dignity to our existence. We can only make some temporary meaning as best we know for our short journey across life's stage. These are all assumptions that flow from the foundational assumption that there is no God and no spiritual dimension. And if we stop and think, many of these assumptions grate us emotionally. (Why these create such emotional discomfort in us needs to be examined. This fact suggests the need for reflection.)

With respect to suffering and the presence of what religion calls "an evil that has a life of its own", the assumption is that all of this is simply the consequence of an unfinished evolutionary process. It will take time; say several hundred thousand more years, for humans to evolve to the place where they have overcome all of these imperfections. It is assumed that the amazing human DNA molecule is on an incredible journey towards perfection. Assumptions all, if we would but stop and examine their foundations!

The Star Trek series and the starship Enterprise illustrated and popularized this evolutionary myth of an advanced human species. Great entertainment, powerfully positive messaging, but that does not make it fact! Such media, together with so much cultural self-talk and cultural circular reasoning, have elevated all of these assumptions to the status of fact. To even question them can cause vehement ridicule because...

D) The atheist, like every other religious person, holds to these assumptions religiously

What does it mean to hold assumptions religiously? These assumptions operate from within the core of our being. They have received the status of unquestioned fact within our hearts. They become part of our identity, if not our identity. We interpret our world and all that happens using these subconscious assumptions. Our interpretation of all our experiences is based on these assumptions. We organize ourselves into tribes or groups or cultures and subcultures based on these assumptions. And, if pushed, we would be willing to die for these assumptions; possibly we would even be willing to kill for these assumptions. All religions, including atheism, can point to such examples in their own history.

Now to elaborate! We interpret our world and our lives on the basis of our assumptions. If we believe in God we will see God everywhere. If we believe in evolution we will see evolution everywhere. This constant circular reasoning reinforces our assumptions continuously and subconsciously. This may be one of the reasons why most conversions from one religion to another happen during youth. A lifetime of circular reasoning has embedded the assumptions so deeply as to be beyond change.

Science has definitively shown that micro-evolution does happen. The claim that macro-evolution happens as well is an assumption based on the fact of micro-evolution. The eagerness with which missing links have been proclaimed as evidence, is evidence of reading theory into facts. Thankfully, true scientists still follow the evidence and all of these missing links have been brought into question. Today's eagerness to find life on distant planets is, among other things, another attempt to show that evolution really happens. If life and, as a consequence, evolution happened on a distant planet, it must have happened here. But again, that conclusion would be an assumption as well!

It does need to be stated that many theistic scientists do believe that evolution is a good way of understanding and interpreting the biological record. But these scientists (some listed under Stone # 8 in Part 5 – Twelve Stones) add that God actively oversaw this evolutionary process till the advent of humankind (and then presumably stopped it). This is far removed from classic evolution that insists that all changes have happened, and are continuing to happen, through accidental mutations. **The issue isn't evolution, but the "God or No God" assumption!**

When faced with facts that seem to contradict our atheistic (or any other religious) assumptions, we will manipulate, ignore, or even deny those facts. We create the spin necessary to support our assumptions.

The atheistic assumptions are beyond argument, beyond doubt. The assumptions have become foundational facts for its adherents. It would usually take a respected outsider to help us become aware that these assumptions exist at the core of our being. It generally takes a major personal crisis for us to critically examine and change our assumptions. If we are an adult it all too often takes a life altering event to force a conversion to another set of assumptions, another religion.

Young adults, on the other hand, are much more open to change because they are naturally engaged with Ultimate Life Question issues during their formative years.

E) Atheism has similarily negative attitudes towards outsiders, non adherents, like every other religion.

Every religion has a place for everyone within their own story line. Every religion is completely **inclusive.** Everyone who has ever lived, everyone who is alive today, and everyone who will come in the future receives a place, a label, within that religion's story line.

Every religion believes itself to be **normative** for all time and all ages. Its position is normal, correct, true by definition. Every other position (past or present) is considered incomplete, abnormal, erroneous, in need of correction. Every religion makes some attempt at persuading these outsiders to conform, to convert to their way of thinking.

Hinduism and Buddhism state that every single living "soul", human as well as grasshopper and angel alike, is on a multi-reincarnational journey to nirvana. They are convinced that eventually everyone will come around to their way of believing. In one of their many reincarnated lifetimes of suffering or seeking enlightenment, everyone will come to the knowledge of the "truth" and reach eternal bliss, nirvana.

Islam labels all outsiders as infidels. In many cultures where civil law is favorable, force is used to convert these infidels. Everyone has only one lifetime. If they convert, well and good! If they refuse, then there is no point in their further existence. They are beyond hope, beyond salvation. It may be a sacred duty to hasten them towards their destiny. These practices, if not official policies, are all too evident in many Middle Eastern cultures today.

Christianity, too, places a strong emphasis on proselytizing, on winning new converts. All outsiders are labeled as unbelievers, destined for an eternity separated from God and everything good. Each person has only one lifetime to make that choice, hence the urgency in the task of evangelism (sharing the good news).

Secular Atheism also believes that it alone has the truth. The ancients pursued various religions to help them "solve" the many mysteries that surrounded them and to help them cope with the fears that permeated their lives. Today, science has "solved" the mysteries and has explained the fears, and as a consequence eliminated the need for religion. All non adherents today are labeled as uninformed, as ignorant, as fundamentalists, as uneducated, as stuck in the dark ages. Not only militant atheism, but culture as a whole is beginning to show more and more frustration with these non-conforming non adherents.

> In 2014 Quebec's ruling political party proposed a "secular" charter. All other religions were to be visibly removed from the public square. It became one of the election issues. Thankfully the party was defeated. Is it just a matter of time till it will become the law of the land? (It is already the practice to a very large degree.)

> Trinity Western University from British Columbia (a Christian University in Langley, BC) has had major court challenges stand in its path in developing an education as well as a law faculty. Popular culture simply cannot have a Christian University become main stream!

Could it be that our secular atheistic cultural institutions have all but marginalized all traditional religious endeavours? Is our culture attempting to force all non adherents into its own religious mold?

F) Every religion, when dominant, shapes its host culture into the "Propoganda Machine" for its belief system.
Religion is not limited simply to the spiritual domain. It touches all aspects of life, from marriage and family to education and ethics, from birth to death ceremonies and everything in between. Religion, after all, provides the worldview, the frame of reference for the ultimate questions and all of their implications for the day to day. Separation of church and

state sounds good in theory and may be necessary in practice (if that were possible) when many religions are vying for allegiance within a multicultural state.

But when one religion is or becomes dominant within a culture then the dynamics change. That religion will begin to transform that host culture so that it reflects its "truth" tenets. That religion will so permeate culture that all opposing views will be marginalized. That religion's "truth claims" will become the popular public understandings. These "truth claims" will seem obviously true within that culture. The resulting circular reasoning reinforces these "truth claims" till they become unquestioned fact.

Circular reasoning needs to be illustrated here. The "religion" is embraced by culture's leaders and its media. These leaders openly teach, speak, and subliminally promote the "truth claims" of that religion. The people within that culture absorb these hidden (or not so hidden) messages. This continues, so often at subconscious levels, till the masses unquestioningly affirm the "truth claims" of the underlying religion as fact. Brainwashed educational institutions and civic functionaries push for ever greater alignment. Any other religion just seems so wrong, so out of step with "reality" as defined by the religion expressed through the vehicle of that host culture. As a result, more aggressive culture shaping continues! (More in Part 4)

Atheism, secular humanism is shaping our culture to an ever greater degree and at an alarming rate. It has become not only the dominant but the dominating view. In matters of sexuality, marriage and family, in matters of conception and euthanasia, it is not simply a slippery slope; it is indeed overt social engineering at the behest of the dominant religion – atheism.

Every religion, when dominant, behaves this way. Atheism is aggressively shaping western culture into conformity to its beliefs system. It is becoming more and more difficult to stand against its influence within culture. This dynamic, so similar to every other dominant religion within its host culture, is added proof that atheism indeed is a religion.

Could it be that "Religion" gets a life of its own? It finds and uses any available method to establish its "truth claims." The education system, best selling authors, the media, the judicial and political system, the artists and the musicians, etc., all are put to use to shape that culture and its unsuspecting people into its image.

We would readily agree that this is indeed happening in every faraway culture and its underlying religion. But could it be that it is happening in our own, while most of us are oblivious to the process?

All cultures and their dominant religious stories act in this same way. The religion creates the unity and the cohesion within that culture. If the prevailing culture and its religion fail to create this unity, polarization and fragmentation happens. Tribalism, "us and them, us and everyone else" mentalities will proliferate and that will eventually destroy the very fabric of that culture.

The growing political divide in the Western World may very well have its roots in the religious stories that the left and the right have as their foundational source. The divide is not only getting wider but deeper as well. That would suggest a deeper subconscious source for the seemingly unbridgeable gap. Is the left following secular atheism's story more faithfully? Is the right following a highly Americanized or Europeanized version of the Christian story? (Would Peter and Paul, James and John, and the many Marys recognize this story? That would make for an interesting debate!)

The melting pot theory of immigration works well for clothes and food and housing. The last aspect of the new immigrants to be "melted, assimilated" into the whole, if at all, is religion.

It could be argued that multi-culturalism is not possible on a practical level. In theory it sounds very good but in practice, that it is another story. Today many sincerely religious people feel that the dominant religion, secular atheism, is using multiculturalism covertly as a smokescreen to preach its own religious perspective. All of its institutions are vigorously shaping the next generation, the immigrants, and the rest of us as well, into its mold, giving other religions little room to maneuver within the mainstream. All public institutions and public spaces allow no mention of god or religion and this falls nicely into the lap of a religion that believes there is no god. Adherents of all other religions fear the loss of their youth. Many are indeed being lost.

Secular atheism presents its own position as neutral, when in fact it is anything but neutral. It is loudly preaching the religion that claims there is no god; at least no god in the traditional sense, not a relational God to whom we must respond, nor a God to whom we are ultimately accountable. But with the impersonal power of evolution on its side, secular atheism, or liberal humanism, proposes an inevitable new world order. Salvation is around the corner! We as humans just need to get with the program i.e. get rid of all the other programs! Christopher Hitchens' book's arrogant title says it all, *God is not great. How religion poisons everything*. According to Hitchen's interpretation of history, all other religions must be eradicated for the good of humanity. He holds to this interpretation religiously!

Some examples of cultural changes that have atheistic values at their very core.

Removal of prayer and Bible reading from public schools (1960's)
Removal of all Religious Studies from schools
Scheduling of major events on Sundays
Removal of Sunday Shopping laws
Removal of Ten Commandments from courthouse laws
Removal of prayer from public venues
Christmas Holidays have become the Winter Holidays – "Merry
    Christmas" is politically incorrect, it is now "Happy Holidays"
BC / AD Before Christ / Anno Domini (in the year of the Lord)
    - This calendar designation recognized Jesus Christ as the
      turning point of global history
    - Changed to BCE / CE (Before Common Era, Common Era,
      or 'Current')
Abortion laws (or lack thereof as in Canada)
Loosening of sexual mores
Redefinition of marriage
Entertainment
    – always pushing the boundaries of social tolerances
Pornography is allowed to become more and more mainstream.
Religion - often the topic of choice for the comedy circuit
Best selling authors - focus is to debunk religion
Euthanasia and Individual Gender choice – the two most
    recent "victories"

Secular atheism, since the 1960's, has been waging cultural war against the then-prevailing religion, Christianity. Is this the reason why modern atheistic cultures seem to have a much more focused agenda against Christianity than against other religions? It almost seems that the new religions coming to our shores have a much easier ride than Christianity. Often, it seems, comments against Christianity would not be politically acceptable if made against Islam.

G) Secular atheism is developing its faith-shaping rituals and liturgies as well

Every religion has its holy sites, its shrines. Every religion develops its own rituals and liturgies to help celebrate its doctrines. Atheism, humanistic materialism has done, is doing, the same.

In medieval Europe the Church was at the physical and cultural centre of every town. The church was the tallest most elaborate building. In western atheistic cultures the Mall, the Stadium, the Entertainment Empire have become the hubs of our cities. These three are the "un-temples" of our culture – places where we "worship" the best humanity has to offer. In our societies these three, with their in-every-home tentacles (TV, computers, media gadgets) have become the fabric of society.

> James K. A. Smith's book, *Desiring the Kingdom* (reading list) has developed these cultural phenomena to a much more excellent degree.

Religion at the Mall

All advertising gurus preach that it is the accumulation of stuff which holds the key to happiness, to the good life. For many, shopping, maybe even just window shopping, has become an addictive ritual. The visit to the mall has replaced the weekly visit to the temple. Some get their weekly fix just buying more stuff, whether needed or not.

Religion by its very definition is the searching for the "good life," usually in some distant future but casting shadows in the here and now. The good life within modern culture is the American Dream, modeled so effectively by our beloved celebrities. The good life for the human DNA molecule lies in the distant future when evolution will have progressed to a much greater degree.

The mall provides everything, and even more, that is needed to enjoy the "good".

Worship at the Stadium.

Youthful bodies in their prime present the best of what it means to be human. Each team has its own cult-like following. To be a fan is to worship at that team's altar. Athletic prowess and multimillion dollar contracts are the keys that unlock religious fervour in the masses. Vicariously, we celebrate their success. Millions of our young people are investing inordinate amounts of money and time and effort with the goal of becoming priest-athlete as well. Their dream is to be worshipped, rather than simply to worship, in the stadium.

The Celebrity Circuit Hyper-Events

Entertainment celebrities all have their cult following. That, by definition, is the key to becoming a celebrity. Each tours the country, if not the world, to stage fantastic self-promoting light and sound spectacles.

It is every person's dream to be "discovered" by the priests of the celebrity circuit. Self-promoting YouTube videos abound. Once "discovered" the priests of the circuit will remold and stage the "lottery winner" into the next Biebs (JB) or Madonna.

Many worship their celebrity. No event has too high a price to pay for whole body and soul "particip-action". Worshippers dress like them, they attempt to talk like them, they memorize their 'quot-able-quotes' and their songs, they attempt to act like them, they buy what they endorse, they decorate their rooms with their posters. It takes religious commitment to unquestioningly support the excesses seen in so much of the celebrity world.

Religion in the Home

Instead of the home altar we have placed the TV Media centre at the most prominent place in the home for that daily in-between go-to fix. For many the solution to the daily problems that weigh us down is simply more entertainment. "Binge-watching" has been added to our vocabulary. We worship the celebrities that parade their talents (or their bodies) across the stage. Our heroes are no longer people of character and valor who have made significant contributions for the well-being of society, but those with celebrity status. Vicariously we enter into their successes. They provide us with the emotional mega fix that we need to get us through our next crisis. They provide us with the ideals (the good life) that become our goals and our purpose for life.

Have the mall experience, the stadium hype, the celebrity events become the religious substitutes within modern culture? Is this where we worship? Is this where we dream? Is this where "the good life" is celebrated? Is this where we get our emotional fix to continue our daily struggles?

All of this may seem rather shallow. Many atheists are indeed looking for more depth.

Religion-less Spirituality

Our culture, it seems, has "successfully" separated conjoined twins, religion and spirituality. Retreats with every imaginable spirituality-without-god disguise are available everywhere, from workshops at career events to wilderness get-aways. (On closer examination many of these events are inspired by eastern religions incognito.)

There is also a move towards more traditional type religious get-togethers to celebrate our humanness. Music, speeches, dances, even formalized liturgies are developing all with the goal of establishing atheism as a legitimate religion for the more sensitive spiritually inclined modern man or woman. A quick search on the internet provides all the help aspiring atheists need to get connected to more traditional religious services and communities. A random sample from the internet follows.

God "less" Church Services for Atheists Go Global

Congregations for atheists are springing up all over the planet. There's already a schism: celebrate life without a deity, or preach atheism. The celebration is winning.

Plans to set up almost 400 "atheist churches" on five continents are underway after the extraordinary success of one small congregation that began holding god-less services just over a year ago.

Word about the religion-free church spread like wildfire after the first Sunday Assembly was held in a deconsecrated church in North London, in January, 2013. By September, 100 congregations will be holding services from Singapore and South Africa to Sao Paulo and San Diego. A further 274 teams currently are working on plans to launch their own assemblies.

http://www.thedailybeast.com/articles/2014/05/04/ godless-church-services-for-atheists-go-global.html

SUMMARY – SECULAR ATHEISM IS THE SAME AS EVERY OTHER RELIGION!

A) Atheism like every other religion has a cosmic story.

B) Atheism like every other religion has a power greater than humanity.

C) Atheism makes foundational assumptions like every other religion.

D) The atheist, like every other religious person, holds to these assumptions religiously.

E) Atheism has similarly negative attitudes towards outsiders, non adherents, like every other religion.

F) Every religion, when dominant, shapes its host culture into the "Propaganda Machine" for its belief system. Atheism is doing the same.

G) Secular atheism is developing its faith-shaping rituals and liturgies as well.

THEREFORE ATHEISM, ALSO KNOWN AS SECULAR HUMANISM OR SCIENTIFIC MATERIALISM ETC. IS A RELIGION!

This discussion has also shown that humans are religious to the core. We cannot function without a religious core, a belief system, at the centre of our lives. The parameters of our belief system can best be understood by examining our behaviors, our life rhythms, our gut-level responses to the many crises of our lives.

No person and no culture is neutral. Every culture is dependent on and has been shaped by its foundational religious story.

In our global community no one is left sitting on the beach. We are all sailing towards a distant shore. A person, or the crowd, may seem to be drifting aimlessly, but in reality they are drifting with the deep currents of the day. We can either consciously set our sails to catch the wind of thoughtfully chosen religious messages or we simply drift with the dominant culture's religious currents.

Just a newsy tidbit to add to the discussion. August 20, 2005

An inmate in a Wisconsin US state prison was hindered in starting a study group for atheists. The court ruled that to deny such a right was to violate the inmate's first amendment rights. (The right to freedom of religion and freedom of expression from government interference.) Atheism, the argument went, was the inmate's religion even though he did not believe in a Supreme Being.

http://www.wnd.com/2005/08/31895/

Mental Climate – Protecting Culture's Meta-Story

Each culture (or sub-culture) has so deeply absorbed its religion, its mother-story, its worldview that the truth assumptions that form the foundation for it are beyond question. The assumptions have unwittingly received the status of fact. To question these assumptions leads to outbursts of heresy or are ridiculed as ignorance. The educational institutions of that culture have unquestionably adopted the assumptions as foundational, as core curriculum, as beyond debate. That culture's legal apparatus has developed the unquestioned arguments and processes needed for supporting those assumptions. All opposing positions are completely ignored, if not publically maligned. This cultural ethos, or mental climate, is easily recognizable in far away cultures, but creates an impregnable blind spot in our own. Here are some well-know examples from our global community, both past and present.

- John Wycliffe (d. 1384) translated the Bible into the language of ordinary men and women, believing that each should be able to examine faith issues on his/her own. He died an outcast of society and his bones were later exhumed and burned as a heretic.
- Martin Luther (d. 1546) was condemned for suggesting intellectual freedom.
- Galileo (d. 1642) was excommunicated from the church for even suggesting that the world was round.
- To even mention anything against Mohammed is cause for the death sentence.

- To suggest that women should be equal to men is considered contrary to reason.
- To float the idea that there might be a personal Creator God is cause for ridicule in the public square.

The mental climate within each of these contexts prevents any reasoned response. The "error" is just too obvious to be even taken seriously.

The net result is that a culture's foundational assumptions are seldom examined with care, either privately by individuals or publicly as a culture. Any opposing viewpoint simply cannot get the traction needed to begin a reasoned debate. Many critical thinkers may need to suffer unjustly before a crack in culture's mental climate appears to allow for some degree of culturally sanctioned examination of the assumptions being challenged.

We would all readily agree with this reasoning when we observe distant cultures and their obvious religious underpinnings. But we rarely consider that the same applies to our own culture and its underlying religion (or un-religion if you insist). A blind spot like no other!

Understanding Fundamentalism

Nothing today causes shivers to go down one's spine quite like the label of fundamentalist. The way our atheistic culture has linked all religion and fundamentalism together as one evil duality is enough to cause people to withdraw from any association with religion. This link needs to be examined.

Defining Fundamentalism: The term fundamentalism, coined in the early 20th century, originally referred to the struggle to cleanse one's own religion from the adulterations that had occurred by the interactions with other belief systems. This form of fundamentalism encourages a return to the original purity of one's faith. The "fundamentals" refers to those articles of faith that a religious group had as its foundational assumptions, the core of their religion, at its launch.

It is naïve to think that fundamentalism in this, its original meaning, will ever disappear. It is the nature of humans and religious faith that causes the assumptions to become hardwired into one's psyche. Every religion will always have its "fundamentalists" (purists) who struggle to regain original purity and with it the original vitality that that religion had when it was birthed and exploded onto the world stage. The energy within this form of fundamentalism is primarily focused on the followers within that religious camp rather than towards those on the outside.

However, today the term fundamentalism has primarily come to refer *to **the attitude of aggressive superiority*** that is conveyed when one assumes that one's own religious assumptions are beyond debate. Any opposing faith positions are judged to be just so out of touch with the "obvious truth". The full extent of the civil law within society is then used to eradicate the opposing sides. (This will be illustrated below.) There may be a lot of truth to the statement, "Bad people do bad things. But it takes religion to make good people do really bad things". The energy within this form of fundamentalism is primarily directed towards outsiders, non-adherents. This type of fundamentalism is the breeding ground for the extremists that seem to be growing within all religious branches.

Recognizing / Resisting Destructive Fundamentalism: Any aware-ness of the history of ideas should cause us all to repeatedly re-examine our attitudes towards those who disagree with us. An awareness of the tremendous suffering that has been caused by respected cultural and religious leaders who have been proven to be so wrong should cause us all to move forward with humility.

We all need to work hard to eradicate the second, the modern version of fundamentalism, the focus on destroying the other, the out-sider, labeled as unbelievers, heretics, infidels, ignorant dinosaurs from a bygone era, etc. This causes tremendous tensions within societies and terrible injustices and wars. The very doctrines of global multi-cultur-alism hope that all the viewpoints and faiths can somehow learn to live together in peace and mutual respect. What is needed if that is ever to be achieved? (This may be very idealistic but nevertheless an ideal to strive for – if societal and world peace is a value we pursue.)

- We need to be deeply aware that our own "truth" position is based on assumptions. Can I identify these assumptions on which I have built my "truth"? Every person, every atheist as well, has them! Most may never have taken the time to identify them. (Appendix C)
- We need to develop the willingness to tolerate each other. We need to learn to agree to disagree without losing respect for the other's humanity. Today's definition of "being intolerant" has evolved to refer to a firm adherent of any religion that claims to be the only way, that claims to have the only truth. (All religions,

including atheism ironically, make such a claim.) This redefinition is an error, intolerance is a behaviour, it must refer to how we treat those who disagree with us.

- We need to learn to really listen to each other, so as to at least begin to understand the worldview of the other.
- We need to learn to express our positions clearly without destroying the dignity and humanity of the other.
- We need to learn to listen to the criticisms leveled against our faith assumptions (and then maybe wait 24 hours) before responding gently and unemotionally to those criticisms.

These steps would go a long way to taking some of the heat out of the debate and restoring reasonable dialogue.

> Could it be that extremism is so much on the rise today because there has been so little real dialogue, so little real discussion on any topic related to religion now that we have become a global community? Would national and trans-national quality forums where people groups can express their ideas and their concerns take some of the steam out of extremism? (Of course one of the pillars of such forums must be to agree to disagree without losing respect for the other.)

Then we simply need to allow the "truth" within each religion, within each culture to speak for itself. After all, each religion, including atheism, believes it has the answers that resolve life's many issues and mysteries. Our lives, our marriages, our families, our communities, our sub-cultures will over time show successes or failures that suggest the degree to which truth lives within our faith story.

FUNDAMENTALISM AND EXTREMISM:

Militant Islam: The global news is replete with examples of aggressive followers of Islam. Many of the wars being fought today seem to be where Islam is pushing its influence into new territory. It is an historical fact that Islam was born in an expansionist and militaristic context and radical Islam is regaining that reputation again. In Islamic cultures we see forced conversions and failing that, public executions, often over-looked, if not sanctioned by the state.

Militant Christianity: Christianity's history is, as well, full of examples of aggressive fundamentalism. The crusades of the Middle Ages are one sorry chapter. The religious wars during the Protestant Reformation are another. Pockets of this pride-filled response to the outsider make great news stories today by our left leaning media. Christianity needs to return to its roots, to the ethics of its founder, where self-sacrificing love was the attitude and the motive behind every interaction with outsiders. Christianity, too, is expansionistic, but when first founded its leader, as well as its followers were invariably on the receiving end of all the hostility.

Militant Atheism: One of Communism's key goals was to eliminate religion, which it defined as the opiate of the people. Churches were destroyed and parents were forbidden to encourage faith in their children; schools systematically, and with vigor, pushed atheism to the younger generations. Tens of millions of people died during Communism's 20th century push to establish their atheistic economic world order. The Communist Revolutions in Russia and China are prime examples of militant atheism.

Today many leading atheists are writing best selling books vehemently denouncing all religious endeavours. Titles like *God is not great, How religion poisons everything* by Christopher Hitchens, and *The God Delusion* by Richard Dawkins are some examples of militant atheism. Thankfully we have civil laws in place to prevent a repeat of

Communism's atrocities; but all other religions have been essentially removed from the public square in our modern "secular" societies by the mental climate created by militant atheism.

Other best selling titles (Amazon's best 10),

Grayling, A. C., *The God Argument: The Case against Religion and for Humanism*, 2013.

Ray, Darrel, W., *The God Virus, How Religion Infects Our Lives and Culture*, 2009.

Have these atheistic authors and their many followers developed an intolerant fundamentalist streak within their own character and in their interactions with non-adherents?

The Problem of Language

Dialogue between adherents of various worldviews is difficult at best, even without all the heat that is typically associated with discussion. One reason is that no one can step outside of his or her own worldview or religion during any discussion. We always speak and listen with a built-in and, too often, personally unrecognized bias. (More in part 4)

Another major problem is that the same word can mean very different things within each of the religions. Careful clarification is necessary, careful listening is essential before any meaningful discussion can even begin.

God
The understanding of "God" is different for each worldview, hence the necessary divisions within religions. (5 differing perspectives on God – 5 different key religions)

> God exalted – transcendent – Islam
> God beside – nearby – Hinduism / animism / North American First Nations
> God within – indwelling – Buddhist Awakening
> No personal, relational God – branches of Buddhism, Atheism
> God all three, exalted, beside, and within (Trinity) – Christianity

In Islam, God is so transcendent, so beyond us in every sense of the word that the only fitting response is total and complete unquestioning submission to him. In Hinduism the one God, Brahman, has so many emanations, is present within all of nature (pantheism), has so many appearances that every worshipper can, if he wishes, have his very own personal close-by god. Each one can have his very own idol for his own god-shelf in his home and for his personal journey through life. In Buddhism, deity, if one is prone to think in terms of the divine, is considered to be within our own souls. "God" is someone to awaken within us all. This awakening, the resulting enlightenment, is therefore the goal of the Buddhist way.

In Christianity we see this combined and conflicting human struggle to understand God brought into a clearer whole. In one sense it is much more mysterious, and yet it is more in keeping with all the clouded insights of our collective human searching. The Trinity, the three in one multi-dimensional God, is indeed the Transcendent One before whom we fall down in worship and submission. In so doing, we sense that he is also deep within us encouraging, enabling, and healing our brokenness. This divine-human embrace is experienced as relationship with another person, who is so very close, so very real, so very personal. The human soul is not lost or diminished (or deified) in the encounter; rather the soul is enhanced, lifted to a higher level of awareness rather than simply the physical plane. Spirituality becomes wholesomely enlivening, deeply enriching, and personally empowering.

C.S. Lewis in *Mere Christianity* (Chapter 24, *The Three Personal God*) has a wonderful chapter on how we can understand and experience this three-dimensional God. (http://www.ldolphin.org/CSLtrinity.html)

The Old Testament suggests this multi-dimensional understanding of God which becomes so much clearer in the New Testament, for example Isaiah 57:14 — 16.

The view that we have of God will inevitably shape our understanding of what it means to be human and what it means to be mature. Our view of God therefore provides the foundational answer to "What is truth?"

Personal Freedom / Maturity

This is the goal that all humanity is striving towards. Each religion though, has a completely different understanding of what it means to have arrived.

In secular humanism, freedom and maturity is the right to do as I please (as long as I don't hurt anyone else). Personal happiness has become the individual's greatest good, culture's greatest idol. When reading or watching popular media today one can almost assume that this has become society's greatest value. This is particularly true of sexual freedom, anywhere, anyhow, with anyone. All inhibitions, it is believed, are remnants of the poisoned fruit of religion and/or bad parenting. Freedom, the pursuit of happiness, is only limited by the principle of not hurting another human being. Science and technology have been tasked to do away with the side effects such as unwanted pregnancies, diseases, inhibitions, cures for any excesses and addictions, etc.

In eastern religions, the goal of freedom and maturity are the direct opposite of secular humanism. Maturity is to be set free from all desires, which are believed to be the root cause of all suffering. Self-denial, the negation of all wanting, is the key to freedom. In these cultures, the ideal is to be an ascetic, to practice and perfect this total self denial.

In Christianity, on the other hand, freedom and maturity are defined as the power to do as I ought. Christianity stresses virtue and character development. It promotes the seven cardinal virtues and discourages the seven cardinal sins.

Cardinal virtues	Cardinal vices
Chastity (purity)	Lust (excessive sexual appetites)
Temperance (self-restraint)	Gluttony (over-indulgence)
Charity (giving)	Greed (avarice)
Forgiveness (composure)	Wrath (anger)
Diligence (zeal. labour)	Sloth (laziness, idleness)
Kindness (admiration)	Envy (jealousy)
Humility (modesty)	Pride (vanity)

84

One does need to ask, which worldview best promotes our humanity? But then, what does it mean to be human?

Human Being

Christianity has a very high view of humanity. According to Christianity we were created as reflections of what God is like. To look at a human being in his personhood, in his moral character is to understand a little of what it means to be God. Humans value true love. God is love. Humans have a screaming sense of justice. God is just. Humans long to be in relationship. God is relationship (Trinity, Three in One, three personalities in relationship and seeking relationship with humanity). Human ethics arise from an enlightened and purified conscience believed to be God's moral standards imprinted on the human soul.

Secular Humanism understands humans simply to be highly evolved animals. We live and die just like animals. There is no spiritual dimension in the traditional sense. Some even go so far as to state that humans have no soul, they are just chemicals interacting. Death is the end. Our lives are ultimately no more significant than those of the animals of the field and forest. Our ethics are to a large extent illustrated for us somewhere in the animal world. Our higher ethics are the product of evolved community consensus. There are no absolutes, no right and wrong, simply because there is no deity. Humans are free to shape morality as they wish.

In Hinduism and Buddhism you and I are disembodied "selfs" on a journey through many incarnations of many different life-forms, from insect to animal to human until the "self" either overcomes the burden of karma or becomes enlightened to awaken the god within. At that point, the "self" is able to be reunited with the universal spirit of God or the Good. Each "self's" individuality will then be "extinguished" or better "perfectly joined with the whole" much like a drop within the ocean.

Salvation: the resolution to the systemic problem of our existence.

Evolutionary science would have us believe that there are as yet genetic imperfections in all life forms. Evolution is as yet unfinished. This is the

CULTURAL AWARENESS

root for all the trauma and suffering within our lifetime. More evolving, say another hundred thousand years or so, is needed to eradicate these imperfections. Sometime in the future we will have evolved more perfect bodies, more wholesome psyches, and will be surrounded by, maybe even "bio-wired" to, a technology that is able to control the uncertain realm of nature. Salvation will be achieved when evolution will have reached a milestone, millennia in the future, when the wilderness within our hearts will have been tamed, and the wilderness outside will have been fully controlled by advances in science and technology.

The Bible, on the other hand, would have us believe that creation indeed was perfect to begin with. Humanity's fall into sin resulted in the loss of the life-sustaining relationship with God. The result is ever increasing failure and brokenness. Evil and sin have left their mark on every aspect of our existence, from our bodies, to our relationships, to the plant and animal world around. What is needed, according to biblical teaching, is a resolution of our sin problem. Salvation will be achieved when the power of Satan and the presence of sin are broken and once and for all removed from the cosmos. Only then will the life-sustaining relationship with God be restored.

Salvation within eastern religions is achieved when the individual soul achieves nirvana. Eternal happiness is achieved when the individual escapes the seemingly endless cycles of birth and death. The world and all its suffering is a needed reality to help the soul overcome karma or achieve enlightenment. The world and suffering will remain as an eternal reality until such a time as every soul reaches nirvana.

We could continue comparing more and more terms to develop a better understanding as to how these classic religions differ. The best way, however, is simply to compare the cosmic stories that lie at their heart. Such basic religious literacy, it seems to me, is essential in our global community.

One of the signs of a great society is the diligence with which it passes culture from one generation to the next. This culture is the embodiment of everything the people of that society hold dear; its religious faith, its heroes... When one generation no longer esteems its own heritage, and fails to pass the torch to its children, it is saying that the very foundation and experiences that make the society is no longer valid.

Stephen Mansfield, *Never Give In: The Extraordinary Character of Winston Churchill*, 1997, page 190.

PATHWAY TO CONFIDENCE

1. Empowering Spirituality

2. Cultural Awareness

3. *Religious Literacy*

4. Validating our Faith Assumptions

5. Encountering the Kingdom Story

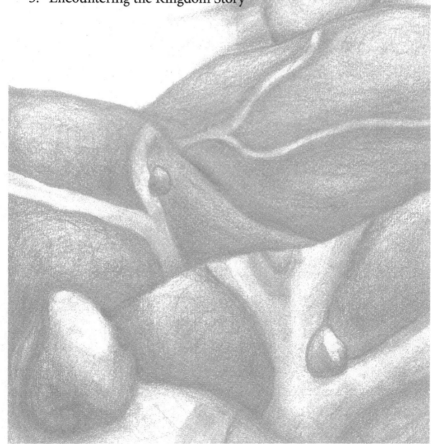

Part 3: Religious Literacy
a few thoughts to begin with...

What follows here in Part 3 is an overview of the world's five major reli-gions, each with its own unique meta-story. Each has developed its own understanding as to how to best visualize the mystery surrounding God. Each has created its own culture and its own mental climate. Each is protective of its own story line, its religion. Each, to varied degrees, seeks to promote its own story line as the one true, the only global story line. This debate will continue as long as the earth and human culture remain.

Too often we read and listen
simply to critique and to reply.
We need to read and listen, first of all,
to learn and to understand.

Introduction to our Tour through the Classic Religions

We live in a global community. Our immigrant neighbours are living a meta-story that may very well be different than our own. They are seeking to keep their meta-story alive as a sub-culture within the larger host culture. Basic religious literacy (foundational understanding of the major religions) should be everyone's goal in today's global community.

A) To begin with, it is necessary to try to understand their meta-story, their mind and heart-set. This will make it a lot easier to understand their perspectives when we are able to enter into conversation with them. That is a necessary first step to help develop respect for them as fellow human beings. They, too, are on a journey. They, too, are ultimately searching for answers to the same questions with which we struggle. The only way to create a more lasting peace and a helpful openness among the religion camps is to foster meaningful, sincere dialogue with a heart-set of humility and mutual respect.

B) Second, it may be very valuable to consider if there is anything we could learn from them that would help us better understand and live our own meta-story. No one lives their own meta-story perfectly. Our perspectives, the glasses with which we are viewing our own religion may have become tinted, if not tainted, by the majority culture around us. A look at our own religion and how we are living its story from the perspective of another religion may very well make us more aware of the blind spots we have developed over time. We may have compromised our meta-story to a significant degree.

> The Judeo-Christian story has its roots in ancient Middle Eastern culture. It is best understood from within that culture. Christianity has been interpreted through western eyes for centuries if not millennia. It is realistic to think that a fresh look from an eastern perspective may uncover many a blind spot.

C) A third reason why a familiarity with the other major stories is helpful, if not necessary, is that we are living in a time when a "create-it-yourself-religion" is becoming the pattern for many. We take what we like from one, a little from another, leaving aside the stuff we do not like. By becoming familiar, we can develop an understanding as to how we have unwittingly borrowed and cobbled together our own set of beliefs. Such a personally cobbled together religious "meta-story" probably will have many internal inconsistencies. (As an example. believing in karma, the progress theme within evolution, meditation so as to awaken the god within, keeping heaven, rejecting any notion of hell, accepting reincarnation, do not agree – they are internally inconsistent. They contradict each other.)

> This internal consistency (internal coherence) is the first step in determining if there is any truth in my own cobbled together story.

D) A fourth reason needs to be stressed. One popular modern day myth states that ultimately all religions are the same. They are all climbing up the same mountain, just from opposite sides. They are all seeking "god" and the "hope" he offers. Even a basic comparative study of the five major religions clearly shows that there is no merit to this modern day myth.

Living in a Global Community

Any discussion with another religion should never contain a pride filled "you are wrong" but a "you too are asking the same questions as we" attitude. Each of the religions has indeed discovered some element of the truth. Much needs to be made of this common ground.

We are all asking the same questions. We all realize that the root problem is a separation from the divine. We all agree that the future (when this separation is resolved) promises to be better than today. We all agree that our behaviour does matter, that how we treat the other is critical. We all, at root, need to be aware that we are building our lives on assumptions that we must accept by faith.

Even the atheist who responds to the above, with a "not us, not us" must be helped to see that they too have created a myopic (short-sighted) religious story of their own. (See a previous section – Atheism is a Religion.)

Confessing that there is much that we can learn from dialogue is the beginning of a new path within our global community. We are all seeking that which makes us whole.

It may be helpful for Christians to meditate on what it means to be a witness to our neighbours. To be a witness is first of all to demonstrate with our lives, our marriages, and our families and communities that the Jesus gospel does make a noticeable difference towards wholeness. It is only secondarily that one uses words to explain to observers the reasons for the changes in our lives and the hope that we do have. If there are no noticeable differences in our lives from those shaped by the dominant culture then no amount of talk will persuade. (For reflection see 1 Peter 3:15.)

As you read the following brief summaries of the world's major meta-stories, try to keep in mind

1) **What does it mean, in the day to day, to live this story consistently?**
2) **How does this meta-story answer Life's Ultimate Questions?**
3) **Is there any wisdom here that may help us in our understanding of the mystery that is the burden of all spirituality?**

Eastern Religions, Foundational Concepts

All eastern religions begin with a completely spiritual interpretation of the world; the material world is in the end an illusion. The strangeness of these understandings to us in the West is understandable because of our over-the-top materialism. In eastern thought, the problem of evil is solved when the self "learns" to detach itself completely from all desires, all attachments to this illusionary world.

The following seven concepts are key pillars of eastern thought. Each of the eastern religions has its own shades of understandings and emphasis.

Atman – The atman is the "self" which is housed in various physical bodies during our many incarnations. The atman is of the same essence as the absolute divine Spirit. This "self" is eternal, indestructible and is at peace only when wed to the Absolute Spirit of the Cosmos. This "self" struggles with duality, with "me and the other" thinking. This "self" may not even really be a soul because that, too, implies separateness from the whole. This duality has robbed the "self" of its place with the Absolute. This duality is experienced as desires and emotions, as a wanting something, a longing for something. Our attachment to the many things and experiences of this world is the root struggle and the ultimate cause of all suffering.

Brahman – This term refers to the Absolute Spirit, the absolute ground of all being. This monism (mono – one) is the belief that there is but one single, indestructible, universal reality. In Hinduism, this Absolute Oneness has qualities, has personality, and as such is represented as the chief God Brahman and his many emanations (derived gods). In Buddhism, this Absolute is without quality, without personality. As such Buddhism is often seen as not having a god. The goal of the Atman, the "self" is to become reabsorbed into this Oneness, this Absolute.

Maya – This term refers to the spiritual truth that this material world and all of its desires and experiences are essentially an illusion. Everything in this world is a distraction from ultimate reality which is found in oneness with the Absolute. Any desiring of something is contrary to the unity in Brahman and as a consequence unreal, an illusion. We need to harness all of our energies to rid ourselves of all our desires, all our addictive attachments to this world.

Kundalini – This is the spiritual energy that rests at the base of the spine, often depicted as a coiled snake. This energy needs to be awakened by a guru, a spiritual leader. This awakened energy is the power behind effective transformative meditation. The yogas, or disciplines, have as a goal, the release of this energy.

Moksha – Release from the struggle, from the endless cycles of birth and death, is moksha. In Buddhism this has been popularized as nirvana. A low level example of release is found in sleep, but here some awareness is experienced in the form of dreams. A higher form of release is found in the waking trance. Those who have disciplined themselves through severe ascetic exercises become increasingly unaware of their surroundings. They have been known to walk through fire or sleep on a bed of nails. The ultimate release found in moksha is when the self has been absorbed back into the Absolute. Complete victory over desire, over time, suffering, birth and death has been achieved. Eternal peace and bliss are then found in the complete realization of "self-less-ness" or "one-ness" with the Ground of all Being.

Karma – All successes or failures prepare us for our next reincarnation. No growth towards moksha is ever lost. No action in our present incarnation is without its consequences in the next. Karma results in much striving: the disciplines of yoga, asceticism, sacrifices, meditation, and temple service, etc. Or, this unforgiving karma results in the reverse, a life-robbing fatalism.

> "We are what we were in the past; we shall be in the
> future what we are now." Hindu proverb

Dharma – Oriental sages prescribed practices and behaviours that provide for the proper functioning of the world and all that is in it. This includes not only the spiritual practices necessary to sustain the spiritual order (temples and priests) but also the cultural order for state, community and family. Normative human behaviors, deduced by the sages through careful observation of nature's ways, are prescribed for all peoples. The cultural understanding of ethics, what is right and wrong, what is righteous and what is evil arises out of these writings. Together they develop a cultural moral common sense. In Buddhism, the Buddha – Dharma is even more comprehensive and provides guidance that leads to enlightenment, to nirvana.

Considerations from a Christian Perspective
There is much that parallels the spiritual truths within Christianity; as well much that moves in contradictory directions. There is much that our western mindset could learn from the eastern mystics.

Similarities
A) To begin with eastern thought has recognized that unity, becoming one with the spiritual Absolute is the goal of all life. This same principle is found in the Judeo-Christian tradition. Reconciliation is the goal of the biblical story as well.

"For God was pleased to have all his fullness dwell in him (Jesus) and through him to reconcile to himself all things, whether things on earth or things in heaven, by making peace through his blood, shed on the cross." (Colossians 1:19-20)

B) Second, the Eastern World has embraced the truth that the spiritual is primary, more foundational than the physical. This is similar in the Judeo-Christian tradition. This truth has been lost in the West; we are all, Christian and non-Christian alike, drowning in materialism. Our greatest challenge is our inability to embrace our spirituality. The West has become spiritually dull, to such an extent, as probably seldom seen before.

C) The East has correctly recognized that less is more. Our addictive obsession to the things of this world, never having enough, always craving more, is the spiritual cancer that is destroying the core of our humanity, and the environment as well. We are consumed with desires that never seem to be calmed. Eastern asceticism would counsel us all, "Want less, calm the desires, above all seek relationship with the Absolute, with God. He is ultimately the only one that can fill the void in our restless heart." The East would encourage a retreating

The church in the west seems to be drowning in materialism just as much as the surrounding culture. The "health and wealth" gospel of so many churches may be nothing more than materialism with a "spiritual" veneer. Could this be one of the reasons for the spiritual shallowness of so much western Christianity today?

from our over-the-top materialism so as to awaken and sharpen our desensitized spiritual sensitivities.

D) The East embraces unity above all else. As a result it stresses contemplation, reverence for the whole. The focus in the East is to hover over a word or concept with the goal of escaping a "this world existence" into a higher form of consciousness. Have we in the West, where the goal is simply to understand through analysis (studying it bit by bit) become stuck in the mundane, the earthly?

So often our approach, as Christians, to the Bible is simply analytical as well. We take it apart so as to understand it, and may in the process lose spiritual connection to the God who is seeking to speak to us. Our goal as we approach the Bible must be to reconnect with God. Relationship, not just analytical knowledge, needs to be our goal.

Differences

A) One significant difference between the eastern religions and Christianity is that the soul's goal is not simply to be absorbed into the divine Absolute, practically disappearing like a drop of water into the ocean. In Christianity we are taught that God values our individuality, our soul, and can save us from our destructive and distracting obsessions, not by negating our individuality but by giving us a new heart. God restores us to himself by giving us his Spirit. We become one with him, not by negating our

According to the Bible God has created the male-female marriage bond to illustrate this Oneness through relationship. We all can envision a marriage relationship where the two have become true soul-mates, separate, healthy, whole individuals but yet perfectly one together, knit together with true love, deep respect, life-long commitment.

individuality, but by becoming reconciled with him (the sin problem effectively removed).

B) Of course the major difference between eastern religions and Christianity is the way the cosmic problem gets resolved. In the East, it is through personal suffering or through enlightenment. In Christianity, it is resolved only through the cross of Christ. Christianity begins with the realization that the problem is beyond human resolution.

Hinduism and its Meta-Story

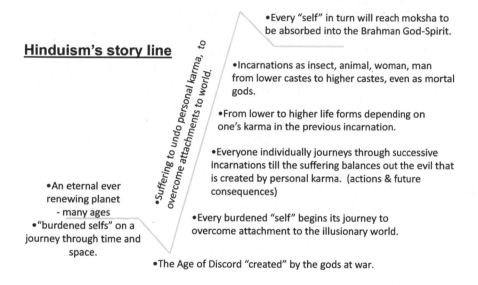

Start to read at bottom left corner

•Each person's last incarnation as an upper caste holy man. A wandering ascetic who has successfully disentangled himself from the illusionary world.

•Every "self" in turn will reach moksha to be absorbed into the Brahman God-Spirit.

Hinduism's story line

•Incarnations as insect, animal, woman, man from lower castes to higher castes, even as mortal gods.

•From lower to higher life forms depending on one's karma in the previous incarnation.

•Everyone individually journeys through successive incarnations till the suffering balances out the evil that is created by personal karma. (actions & future consequences)

•Suffering to undo personal karma, to overcome attachments to world.

•An eternal ever renewing planet - many ages
•"burdened selfs" on a journey through time and space.

•Every burdened "self" begins its journey to overcome attachment to the illusionary world.

•The Age of Discord "created" by the gods at war.

The world is eternal and continually in flux, repeatedly degenerating and then being renewed again. The present age is called Kali Yuga or the Age of Discord. The world will remain until every "self" has experienced moksha. No one will lose out on eternal bliss, eternal Oneness with the Universal Spirit of Brahman.

This meta-story has a strong practical individualism. To aid another soul in its suffering may be counter productive. Karma dictates suffering and to alleviate it may require a repeat incarnation. Each self, burdened by karma, journeys through many lifetimes (some have estimated over

600,000 lifetimes, from insect to mammal to human etc.) till moksha, complete awareness of Oneness with Brahman, is experienced.

Hinduism's culture

Hinduism is the oldest of the classic global religions, ca. 2000 BCE. Hinduism seems to be a synthesis (a coming together) of India's many ancient religious traditions. We find many variations within Hinduism but each has similar basic philosophical underpinnings. This religion is based on the early writings of a multitude of Vedic sage-poets. The belief systems have seen continuous evolution and in the process have spawned many other oriental religions like Buddhism in the 5th century BCE to Hare Krishna in the 15th century CE.

Hare Krishna is a movement that became popular in New York during the spiritually turbulent years of the 1960's. Hinduism's playful and amorous (lover) god Krishna was elevated to the highest status within the pantheon of gods. Hare Krishna seems to be a reaction to the severe asceticism of Hinduism.

The earliest sacred writings of the sages are called Veda (Knowledge). Later religious writings are captured in the Upanishads and Bhagavad Gita. A person becomes a Hindu by repeating a sacred mantra in the presence of a guru from the sect which the person wants to join.

In India, Hindu culture is marked by a rigid caste system. A person's birth into a particular caste is determined by the moral progress (karma) achieved in previous reincarnations.

Brahman – priest caste
Kshatriya – rulers and warriors
Vaisha – commoners (traders, merchants and farmers)
Shudra – servants - the lowest

Each caste can be broken down into even more divisions. The caste system permeates all of Hinduism's social structure. Will the pressures of modernization stress this rigid social structure sufficiently to cause foundational cultural change? (The privileges of the upper caste and the glass ceiling of the lower classes have been linked to karma for millennia.)

Hinduism is permeated with polytheism (many gods). Every family has its chosen god and a god-shelf within the home. Some of the more significant gods have large followings. Many of the sects have special facial markings and they build and worship at elaborate temples. All the various idols are considered emanations or representations of the Universal Brahman Spirit. Religious practices include temple building, sacrifices (chiefly vegetarian), pilgrimage, asceticism, and the yogas (meaning the disciplines). All religious practices are an inward searching to awaken humanity's deeper spiritual powers so as to help overcome the desires and attachments that are at the root of all suffering. The goal is always to improve one's karma for the next reincarnation.

Typically four life stages are suggested for each human reincarnation.
Learner, student
Householder, carrying responsibilities for family and career
Forest dweller, "retirement" set aside to meditate on spiritual truths
Ascetic – at this stage the world has been renounced

The first three stages are governed by Dharma (rules that govern social order). The last is considered beyond Dharma, beyond good and bad.

LIFE'S ULTIMATE QUESTIONS
FROM HINDUISM'S PERSPECTIVE

- The Question of Truth – The Foundational Question.
  - Truth is found in the writings of the ancient sages. These sayings are at times considered revealed, at other times the words of the very wise.
  - God is the ultimate personal Spirit of the cosmos. Our heart's greatest need is to again become one with this God-spirit.

- The Questions Surrounding our Humanity.
  - A human is simply one of the many reincarnations of the self.
  - Overcoming desires, wanting less, becoming an ascetic is of great value in improving one's karma for the next reincarnation.
  - Male is a higher reincarnation than female - better karma.

- The Question of Ethics.
  - Careful observation of nature and life as it happens around us provide understanding of the dynamics that make life better.
  - Dharma, the careful reflections by the sages, provides the guidelines for all of life: family, community, and kingdom.

- The Questions Surrounding Evil and Suffering.
  - All suffering within one's life is the result of karma from previous reincarnations.
  - In Hinduism, (as well as Buddhism) there is no great moral problem with a God who is all-powerful as well as all-good. The need to achieve detachment explains the necessity of suffering. God is off the hook!

- The Questions Surrounding the Future.
  - Multiple reincarnations await after death. More and more suffering, more and more effort to overcome karma.
  - The goal is to escape the birth and death cycle and become one with the Absolute Oneness, the Brahman Spirit.

It needs to be noted that in the East reincarnation is the curse of our existence, the reality that needs to be overcome. In the West, reincarnation has been popularized (Americanized?) as something positive and desirable. What is the "evidence" that supports these faith assumptions?

HINDUISM AND THE WESTERN CHURCH

The western church is rightly concerned with all the idolatry in the East. Many deities, from the River Ganges (to bathe in its waters is to become pure), to Shiva (the god of destruction and transformation), to all the personal deities of every home's sacred shelf, has led to an over the top polytheism.

We in the West have our own "idols" as well. From celebrity cult followings to extreme sports, to sports fanaticism in the extreme, from the latest fashion fads to the latest ideologies, from the latest gadgets to bucket list experiences, as well as our many addictions, all are so prone to take centre-stage in our lives. Anything that takes our priority focus away from our relationship with God could very well be defined as an idol. If these idols form the centre around which our lives revolve, we are on a detour and heading in the wrong direction no matter if we are from the East or from the West.

104

Buddhism and its Meta-Story

Start to read at bottom left corner

•Each person's last incarnation as a Buddha, a holy man, spends a lifetime praying for souls trapped in the cycle of birth, suffering, and death.

•Every soul in turn will reach nirvana to be absorbed into the Absolute like a drop of water into the ocean - eternal supreme happiness and peace.

Buddhism's story line

Theme: Achieving Enlightenment.

•Ever higher levels of incarnations - more suffering, more meditation, greater degrees of awakening.

•Meditation, emptying, calming the mind, avoiding extremes, extinguishing desire.

•From insect to animal to woman to man.

•An eternal ever self-renewing planet.
•"Deluded selfs" on a journey through time and space.

•Everyone on the journey through successive incarnations till the soul is awakened, enlightened.

•Every ignorant soul begins its journey to become enlightened.

Buddhism's meta-story is similar to all eastern religions. Every "self" is on a journey towards Moksha, towards release from the endless cycle of birth, suffering and death. This escape from the illusionary world is called nirvana. The earth is eternal and will remain until everyone has become a Buddha (a teacher for all the rest of us) during their last incarnation, and then into nirvana after that last death.

Buddhism originated in Northern India in the 6th century BCE. It seems to be a response to the excesses of Hinduism.

- No longer a fatalistic focusing on overcoming karma from previous incarnations, the goal is positive, overcoming ignorance, achieving enlightenment.
- Hinduism's over the top idolatry has been replaced by a focusing on the inner light. If one is prone to think in terms of deity, "god" is within. The "god spirit, the universal principle", is without personality.
- Hinduism's excessive asceticism is replaced with the path of moderation, avoiding the extremes of asceticism on the one hand and self-indulgence on the other. The smiling meditative Buddha statues that dot the landscape and the temples illustrate this gentler approach to life.
- Like the principle of karma, no growth towards enlightenment is ever lost, it shapes the next incarnation. Suffering is necessary to encourage growth towards enlightenment.

The narrative begins with the story of its first enlightened Buddha...

Siddhartha Gautama prepared for his last incarnation by performing many acts of generosity and self-sacrifice. Many stories of the 2nd to last, and his many previous incarnations, have been collected; they read like fables for teaching ethical lessons of kindness and goodness. His very last incarnation consisted of a birth into a royal family in Northern India. He grew up in the palace, was educated as a prince, married, and had a child. At age 35 he saw 4 visions (a sick person, an old man, an ascetic and a corpse) which provoked a radical change of direction for his life. He renounced his status and his wealth and became a wandering monk. He attempted to find happiness through asceticism. Failing this, he chose the middle path, neither self-denial nor self-indulgence. He embarked on an in-depth period of meditation under the Bohdi tree, the tree of wisdom, to once and for all find the solution to the suffering in the world. It was under the Bohdi tree that he experienced his awakening. He awoke from the deep sleep of ignorance that binds all living things to the suffering of the world. He became the first Buddha!

He continued living as the Awakened One, as the Buddha, and taught the secrets he had discovered till age 80, at which time he died peacefully, never to be born again. He had achieved nirvana. All his followers await their turn to become a Buddha, an enlightened one, and then enter into that eternal state of bliss.

Buddhism has developed the four noble truths and the eightfold path as the pathway of wisdom. Buddhism's goal is to avoid all extremes, to always find the middle road. This is the path that creates the greatest potential for peace within one's heart and mind, within community and culture. This middle road reduces the suffering that is so prevalent. The suffering that we experience is simply there to encourage us to pursue the wisdom of the 4 noble truths and the 8 fold path, the goal being to achieve enlightenment, to enter nirvana.

The four noble truths
    Suffering exists
    There is a reason why suffering exists
    There is a way to end suffering
    The way to end suffering is through the eightfold path

The eightfold path
    Right views – understanding the 4 noble truths
    Right thoughts – letting go of wants and desires
    Right speech – telling the truth, speaking wisely and kindly
    Right action – no cheating or stealing
    Right livelihood – an honest living that does no harm
    Right effort – encouragement and endurance to keep the 8-fold path
    Right mindfulness – being aware how my actions and words
        impact others
    Right concentration – peaceful state of mind through practice of the
        8-fold path

Buddhism is one of the world's great missionary religions. From India, Buddhism spread through all of Asia. In many of these oriental cultures Buddhism is practiced alongside the local religion. In many it has morphed into a new eastern religion.

- Zen Buddhism developed in China and Japan. The focus is on meditation for the purpose of practical application rather than simply spiritual learning. The principles of cause and effect in the day to day are a key focus.

Adherents are encouraged to set aside some time (months, even years) for serious meditation in the many monasteries within the land. These bands of monks, to a degree, live off the charity of common folk. The shaved heads, the typical orange robes all encourage the negation of individuality, which is necessary for becoming one with the Absolute Oneness of the Cosmos.

Buddhism continues to expand through its missionary activities. The Dali Lama, the leader of Tibetan Buddhism, has travelled the world and has received a particularly warm welcome in the West. Possibly Buddhism's tendency towards not having a god meshes well with western atheism. Its One Unifying Universal Spirit is without personality, without qualities. "God" is within us all and needs to be awakened through meditation, through the 8 fold path. Buddhism's focus on becoming enlightened parallels the West's emphasis on education. Possibly the West's hollow or shallow spirituality is fertile ground for just such a seemingly nonconfrontational missionary movement.

Many in the West are turning to the disciplines of the Buddhist path. The need to calm the mind, to stop the mind-games that magnify so much stress, that create so much hypertension, is well illustrated by the following observation made recently. A typical young man, sitting at a table at a fast food establishment, a large coffee within reach (caffeine kick and who knows how much sugar), a cigarette in the one hand, an iPhone in the other, texting away, headphones over ears, head bobbing to the beat of heavy music. With so much mental stimulation (addictive?) one can well imagine the need for mind discipline (called mindfulness in contemporary westernized Buddhist literature) later in life just to be able to calm the nerves, to be able to settle so as to sleep, never mind succeed in career. Buddhism, adapted to western culture, will inevitably find desperate seekers.

> "Global marketing communication giant JWT named mindfulness one of its *Future 100: Trends and Change to Watch in 2015.* According to the annual report, "Meditation and mindfulness are getting mass appreciation for benefits not just in well-being, but also in work success—and being embraced by young urban audiences from Silicon Valley to Manhattan."

> *Making Money from Mindfulness* by Rieva Lesonsky, *Growing Your Business,*

> Published March 26, 2015 , *FOXBusiness.*

The Bodhi Tree Dharma Center. Come, relax and be. We are a place where you can meditate in a beautiful, quiet setting and develop the capacity for unconditional dedication to the service of others with mindfulness for individuals, families and communities.
Used with permission
Drawn by Hailey Friesen CCS grad 2016

LIFE'S ULTIMATE QUESTIONS
FROM BUDDHISM'S PERSPECTIVE

- The Question of Truth – The Foundational Question.
    - Truth is found in the story of, and the writings of, the first Buddha and the ancient sages.
    - "God" is within. To awaken this "god-spirit" is to become one with the Universal Ground of all Being.

- The Questions Surrounding our Humanity.
    - Life is all about achieving enlightenment, awakening the "god within".
    - Life is about improving one's moral standing, one's karma for the next life.
    - Both male and female can be monks – equal karma?

- The Question of Ethics.
    - The sayings of the sages (Buddha – Dharma) provide the guidelines for all of life, family, community, and kingdom as well as help towards enlightenment.
    - These sayings, often the result of careful observation of nature and its ways make life better.

- The Questions Surrounding Evil and Suffering.
    - Evil is the result of ignorance, the lack of enlightenment.
    - Human desiring, our attachments to this world, are the cause of suffering.
    - All the suffering within one's life is an incentive to seek enlightenment.

- The Questions Surrounding the Future.
  - Multiple reincarnations await after death, as well as more and more suffering and more and more discipline to achieve enlightenment.
  - The goal is to escape the birth and death cycle and become one with the Absolute Oneness, the Ground of all being.
  - The world will continue (history is circular) till all have reached nirvana.

CONSIDERATIONS FROM A WESTERN PERSPECTIVE

There is much wisdom for life here. To seek the middle road is a truth from which we in the West could surely benefit.

The Eight-fold Path's challenge to repeatedly refocus on that which is most important is surely advice we desperately need. We all too often measure our lives by the number of distractions that we can cram into our days, and in the process lose all sense of calm and direction for our lives. (To what degree do we as Christian churches reflect the same busyness, the same noise, the same cultural rhythms of distraction and excess?)

Buddhism's focus on inner enlightenment, on awakening the "god within" parallels the West's emphasis on education. It should be no surprise that many in the West are turning to Buddhism. The focus on the "inner light" rather than a "God out there" is more palatable to a generation that has been shaped by atheism. How much of the burgeoning modern day spirituality without religion movement is Buddhism incognito?

A theme for reflection: can enlightenment, or education alone, solve the deep moral issues within our lives? To what degree do we need an infusion of resources not available within?

In the West we strive to avoid suffering by whatever means available, from a pill for every pain to euthanasia. Can suffering have a positive effect in our lives? Is suffering necessary in order to discover the secrets of life?

Introduction to the "Revealed" Religions

Judaism, Christianity and Islam all claim that God has spoken through prophets to humanity. Answers to life's ultimate questions can only be found in God and in his self-revelation. These "revealed" religions clearly state that all of humanity's seeking after ultimate truth (our many religious pursuits) is doomed to confusion and uncertainty. Science does, these religions teach, give answers to the physical world but cannot begin to understand the much more important spiritual dimension.

All three revealed religions are Abrahamic in origin. All three claim Abraham as their spiritual father. Judaism and Islam claim Abraham as their physical ancestor as well, children of Isaac and Ishmael respectively. All three are longing for their "Messiah" to come and resolve the issues plaguing our existence.

Judaism began with Moses and the giving of the Torah (the first 5 books of the Old Testament) around 1400 BCE.

Christianity began with the coming of Jesus Christ into the Jewish story. Christianity, through the New Testament, boldly proclaims that Jesus is the long awaited Jewish Messiah.

> According to Christianity, the Jewish people, as a nation, misunderstood the nature of the Messiah's mission and as a result rejected Jesus during that first century so long ago. Many Jewish people did accept Jesus as their Messiah and became part of the Christian Church. For the first few

decades the church was primarily Jewish. According to Christianity, Jesus first came to solve the spiritual problem for all of humanity. The New Testament, the foundational book for Christianity, must be seen as a thoroughly Jewish writing by Jewish authors (only Luke-Acts was written by a Gentile). The New Testament can only be correctly understood within the culture of the Old Testament.

Islam began with Mohammed and the Koran, in 623 CE. Islam builds on the Jewish and Christian prophetic and Messianic traditions. It is believed that Mohammed's final successor will come for the great culminating battle when evil is finally removed and when full and complete righteousness is restored into the human story.

At best, only one of these religions can be true, the other two are adulterations. But which ones?

It must seem so tempting for any outsider who observes the contradictory truth claims within these three related "revealed" religions to simply walk away in disgust. One thing, however, needs to be taken into account. Within these three traditions we read about the presence of personal evil. The focus of this satanic power is to frustrate God's good plans for this planet by destroying the human family. If Satan cannot do away with the truth, it could be expected that his next strategy would be to muddy the waters with respect to that truth. This, Satan has indeed successfully done.

But we have reason to hope. If God is indeed all powerful and all loving, as all three insist, then one would expect that God would make it possible for humans to find their way. We can, with sincerity and humility of heart, prayerfully find our way through the confusing labyrinth of these competing religious truth claims. The evidence lies within their origins, their histories, within their scriptures, and with the impact that true adherence generates within the human heart and within the human community.

These three related religions are linear rather than circular. (Eastern meta-stories are cyclical, the world will continue, age after age, until every self has reached nirvana.) In these "revealed" religions, the story is singularly moving towards a climatic event, the visitation of God's Messiah himself to once and for all resolve the existential issues plaguing humanity's existence. Each of these religions boldly proclaims that their Messiah will appear and with him the root issue plaguing mankind will be resolved.

This internecine (inter family) feud, as to which of these three related spiritual traditions is the truth, will only be solved when this long-awaited Messiah actually does return.

114

Islam and its Meta-Story

Start to read at bottom left corner

•The Mahdi, the Enlightened One, descendant of Mohammed, conquers decisively, establishes the worldwide Caliphate.

Islam's story line

•Restoring Allah's rule, Sharia law which leads to global peace and harmony.

•Resurrection & Judgment Day
•Paradise or heaven for the faithful, eternal torment for the infidels.

• Epic fights, Jesus returns, is aligned with the Mahdi, catastrophic earthquakes, global chaos.

•Mohammed, the final prophet comes, receives the seal (completion) of the prophetic tradition. The Koran is given as Allah's final word.

•Jesus comes as a major prophet, is rescued from the cross, is taken into heaven for end time service to Allah.

•All the heroes of the Bible are prophets and/or messengers from Allah.

•In the beginning Allah
A good creation
Humans created as Allah's successors, subjects.

•The prophetic tradition begins. Repeatedly more prophets are sent to encourage people to submit to Allah.

•Satan refuses to honour Adam and Eve. He tempts them. They disobey but do repent. All descendants are born good but struggle to submit just as Adam and Eve did.

HISTORY OF ISLAM

Islam exploded onto the world stage during the 7th century among the Arabian coastal and desert clans. Mohammed, the founding father of Islam, lived during a time of rich religious diversity. Many local tribal religious traditions, Jewish settlements, as well as large pockets of Christianity, co-mingled and added to the fragmentation of the unruly and fierce Arabian tribes.

Religiously, Mohammed (ca. 570 - 632 CE), through his 20 year span of supernatural revelations (the Koran), was successful in creating a dynamic, unified whole out of the smorgasbord of religious ideologies that existed on the Arabian Peninsula.

Militarily and politically, Mohammed's unprecedented success was to create a political unity among these diverse tribal sheikdoms. The birth of Islam accomplished what must have seemed impossible during the centuries prior. These extraordinary successes propelled Islam's rapid march beyond the borders of Arabia and into the world. Within 300 years of Mohammed's death, Islam had gained military victories throughout the Middle East, into Africa, India and even into Europe. Today its largest concentration lies in the Far East, in Indonesia. This last expansion was primarily through trading relationships and the many intermarriages between the Muslim traders and the local people. Not only does this rapid geographical expansion astonish, but the fact that Islam as a religion put down permanent and lasting roots in these occupied territories is without comparison. All are accomplishments of the first order.

It does need to be noted that during Islam's zenith at the turn of the millennium (1000 - 1200 CE) all the subdued countries and ethnic groups, including the Jews, enjoyed a degree of peace and prosperity under their Islamic overlords. This needs to be compared to the backwardness of the Christian nations to the north during that same time period. Much of the learning that fueled the European Renaissance a few centuries later had been carefully preserved in the Islamic Middle East.

HISTORY IN CONTEXT — THE CRUSADES 1096-1272 CE

Christian Europe's attempt at freeing the holy lands from the Islamists consisted of nine military campaigns over several centuries. Papal power struggles (e.g. religious authority vs King's authority), religious fervour, the papal promise of forgiveness of all sins, the promise of adventure and treasure inspired hundreds of thousands to volunteer. The only crusade that met with a degree of success was the first one. Many were military disasters for the Christian forces. The last turned out to be a power struggle within the divided "Christian" church, the Roman Catholic against the Eastern Orthodox. How many of the modern day tensions between the East and the West have their roots in these misguided conflicts?

The church, wed to the state as it was, misunderstood the nature of the Kingdom that Jesus came to bring. The Kingdom of Heaven is birthed within the human heart rather than in empires built by the sword and housed in brick and mortar castles.

Jesus said, "My kingdom is not of this world." John 18:36

THE RELIGIOUS ROOTS OF ISLAM

The religion of Islam has "borrowed" significantly from the ideologies present within the Arabian subcontinent. It has created a new religion that has successfully superseded them. Islam has captured a medieval orthodoxy that has survived to our day. The present day growing Islamic push to return to its original purity and vitality has put the whole world on notice.

Islam's radical monotheism (one God), and its hope for a Messiah, have their roots in Judaism.

Allah was the name of a local supreme deity of Mohammed's local Bedouin tribe. The Kaaba in Mecca, the focal point of today's once-in-a-lifetime Islamic pilgrimage, was the centre piece of a local tribal annual festival. Muslims believe it to be the first House of Allah built by Abraham.

Mohammed's first task upon conquering Mecca militarily was to cleanse this holy site of all its pagan idolatries. Mohammed's bold proclamation of pure monotheism successfully eliminated all other tribal deities.

All the main characters of the Hebrew Bible are absorbed into, and deemed prophets and messengers, within Islam. The gospels of Jesus (called the Injil) have as well been adopted into the collection of Islamic sacred writings.

In an ingenious masterstroke, Islam presented itself not simply as an upstart antagonist to the other religions around, but as the completion (and cleansing) of all their collective traditions.

ISHMAEL OR ISAAC – THE ARABS OR THE JEWS AS ALLAH'S CHOSEN PEOPLE?

According to Islam, Judaism had in error taken upon itself the title of the favoured Abrahamic son. The Jews had, by corrupting the Torah (Old Testament), stolen the birth right and with it the dignity of the Arabic tribes. Is it any wonder that there is such tension between the Arabic peoples and the Jews to this day!

According to Mohammed, it was Ishmael, the father of the Arabs, not Isaac, the father of the Jews, who received the title of "first born". Ishmael had been given the sacred trust to carry the tradition forward. With the stroke of the pen, the birthright was restored to Ishmael, the father of the Arabs, and it was only fitting that the last and greatest of the prophets should have come through Ishmael's line.

It was during the first three Islamic centuries that many stories surrounding Mohammed's life were collected. He became more and more a man of undiminished character and unsurpassed wisdom, a most successful leader, politically, militarily, culturally, and above all spiritually, who displayed all the virtues most admired by all Muslims. (How many of these stories are true and how many are edited is a question that would contradict the reverential honour due to this most eminent prophet.)

THE KORAN AND THE HADITHS

The Koran, literally a collection of recitals, the chief of all scriptures, is proclaimed as an exact dictation from God's heavenly book of books. Earlier writings, those from the Old and New Testament, had been imperfectly received and had become so corrupted that humanity needed a final accurate dictation to seal divine revelation once and for all. Is it any wonder that any negative word against the Koran, or against the final prophet through whom God spoke, is punishable by death! It is deemed to be mankind's most sacred responsibility to keep this final revelation from Allah in impeccable and irreproachable condition.

The Koran is the most significant unifying power for the Muslim people worldwide. It is believed to be the very presence of Allah within the community. The Koran is never to be placed on the ground. A personal cleansing rite precedes the handling of a copy. Tradition often suggests that words from the Koran be the first words to be whispered into the newborn's ear. It is the first and the chief of all books within Islam's educational culture. It is a most worthy goal to commit the Koran to memory even when Arabic is not one's mother tongue. The five daily prayers are to a large degree recitals from the Koran. Sections of the Arabic text are chanted at all community events and festivals as well as all rites of passage. It has been copied and printed through the centuries with the most embellished calligraphy. Copies are works of art to the highest degree. Words from the Koran are used to adorn public buildings and architecture. The Koran has indeed shaped the culture and the heart-set of the people.

The Koran, about the length of the New Testament, proved to be insufficient for the governance of all the territories newly conquered after the prophet's premature death. During the next three centuries, great effort was made to collect all the traditions of the prophet and his original community. These traditions, six volumes in total, called the Hadiths, are second in importance within Islam. Great emphasis is placed on keeping the traditions of the prophet within all of community and family life. This emphasis is the fire within Islam today. A return to pure Islam, it is believed, will see a return to its original vitality and power. And this renewal will usher in the worldwide Islamic Caliphate.

SUNNI OR SHIA, ARABIA OR IRAN

The Sunni and Shia divide is the greatest historical schism within Islam. The issue centers on leadership within the movement. The Sunni, based in Arabia, believe that the mantle of leadership falls on the elected or appointed successors to Mohammed. The Shia, based in Iran, contend that leadership rests on the Ayatollahs from the family lineage of Mohammed. Which is the correct tradition? This question is one of the roots of the internecine (inter-family) struggles within the Middle East today. The present day political power struggle between Arabia and Iran has its roots in this question of leadership.

TRUTHS "CORRECTED AND SEALED"

Many significant differences are to be noted between Islam and its Judeo-Christian forerunners. Many of the challenging issues, believed to be corruptions, within the Judeo-Christian Bible have been "corrected." Many of the Jewish and Christian truth claims that had created such debate and controversy before they were finally settled during the great Church councils of the early centuries have been eliminated. Islam did successfully make itself more palatable, more acceptable, to the early medieval human mind and heart.

The Nature of Sin

In Judaism, and in particular Christianity, the human fall into sin is emphasized. Humankind, it was taught, had become so depraved, so corrupted during the Genesis 3 Garden of Eden fall, that the bent towards evil was present in everyone, right from birth. In Islam we read that no such thing as original sin exists. Everyone is born perfect with a bent towards Allah. Humanity's difficulty lies in the fact that it forgets, or is tempted, or is too stubborn, to do Allah's will. Humanity just needs constant reminders, constant correction, hence the prophetic traditions, hence the prescribed five pillars (see below) of Islamic culture.

The Understanding of God – the Trinity
The Christian mystery of the Trinity, the Three in One God, is eliminated in the Koran. Allah is one, and Mohammed is his chief and final prophet. Jesus is now accepted simply as a prophet of distinction among the many who preceded Mohammed. Allah is beyond even the notion of having a son. One indivisible, magnificent and transcendent Creator God, to whom the only fitting response is complete and unquestioning submission, clarifies the mystery surrounding the teachings of the Supreme Being.

The Cross of Christ
Christianity is fixated on the crucifixion of Jesus. This "bloody corruption" is eliminated in Islam. According to the Koran, Jesus did not die on the cross but was rescued and taken up into heaven by Allah. (Jesus will return as servant to Mohammed's glorious descendant when this meta-story reaches its end time conclusion.) The death of Jesus was not needed to pacify Allah's wrath at humankind's sin. Allah does not get angry. Allah is merciful and more than willing to forgive humanity's sinful forgetfulness when humans simply resubmit to him. No such sacrifice for sin has ever been necessary.

Holy Spirit Mysticism
The mystical elements within Christianity have been removed by Islam. No new birth is necessary. No Holy Spirit is needed to bring new life to the supposed spiritual deadness within the human heart. In Islam, conversion is effected simply by repeating the Shahadah, "There is no God but Allah and Mohammed is his prophet", and acknowledging the key beliefs of the Koranic worldview. The mystical notion of the indwelling of the Holy Spirit within the human heart is a corruption according to the Islamic teaching. The Holy Spirit as the third person of the Trinity is eliminated. These unexplainable supernatural elements within

Christianity that so often created such confusion for converts and longtime adherents alike have been removed. The Christian emphasis on a relationship with deity, so often experienced as so mysterious, so complex and so messy has been eliminated in favour of a simple unquestioning submission to, and acceptance of, Allah's will as it unfolds in all of our circumstances.

One larger branch within Islam, Sufism, has developed many particularly emotion-filled traditions. Passionate veneration of Mohammed and the Koran, expressed in dance, poetry, music, and art satisfies the deeper needs within many a human heart for emotional and trance-like religious expression.

THE FIVE PILLARS THAT SHAPE FAITH AND CULTURE

Islam, as a religious system, has mastered the role of extrinsic, externally induced transformation. Mandated routines, repeated often, shape the believers towards the Islamic mindset and lifestyle. It is this that has created a sense that Islam is the religion of law and legislation. Over time the believers develop the intrinsic convictions that internalize the faith.

Salat – Daily prayers repeated five times: at sunrise, noon, in the afternoon, at sunset and bedtime. The calls to prayer are chanted from every mosque's minaret at the designated times. Constant daily reminders to pray, to prostrate oneself and to chant the appropriate Koranic citations are seen and heard in every Islamic village. At the workplace, in the home, wherever one finds oneself, everything stops for the mandated prayers. The prayer rug is always within reach.

Shahadah – "There is no God but Allah and Mohammed is his prophet." Every Muslim repeats this confession often.

It is the beginning and end of every prayer as well as an oft repeated recitation within Islamic culture.

Alms giving – the giving of a regulated portion of one's income (2.5%) for the provision of the poor within the communities.

Ramadan – Annual month-long fast – no food or drink between sunrise and sunset. Many large community worship events are held to commemorate this holy month. The giving of the Koran began in this month.

Hajj – Pilgrimage to Mecca – It is obligatory for all Muslims of sufficient means to travel at least once to this holiest of sites within the Islamic religion. This pilgrimage to the Kaaba in Mecca, with its many community ceremonies, is often a significant, religious, life changing, mystical experience for many Muslims.

And given the anticipated nearness of End-Time fulfillment

Jihad – resisting evil (struggle, effort), to begin with the evil within oneself, and then actively pursuing the worldwide Islamic Caliphate through all culturally acceptable means. (whose culture?)

ISLAMIC MINDSET AND CULTURE

Islam simply means to submit. Muslim refers to any person who islams. The mosque literally means the place of prostration. Friday is set aside as the day of gathering, of saying the prayers within the mosque in the context of community. Friday prayers conclude with a message from the Imam, the leader within the local mosque.

The traditional Islamic prayers involve a bowing from the waist, followed by kneeling, and then placing the forehead on the ground. The repetitive words of the Shahadah and other Koranic texts, the body repeatedly prostrated, the direction towards Mecca, all within the context of community, all harmoniously and continuously reinforce the notion of total submission to deity. This is humanity's purpose and obligation: to humbly, unquestioningly submit to the sovereign will of Allah as it plays itself out in one's own life.

Many observers of cultures have noted a tendency towards fatalism within the heart-set of a people so shaped, a resignation to the circumstances one finds oneself in. It is often difficult for Islamic communities to engage in constructive changes to alleviate pain and suffering, simply because one's situation is deemed to be Allah's will. (Parshall, 130)

THE ISLAMIC META-STORY

According to the Islamic worldview, this religion, "revealed" in the 7th
century, began in the beginning with Adam and Eve. Allah created the
world and all of its inhabitants. Allah's one supreme requirement for
humanity was that they submit to his sovereign will. In this meta-story,
Allah is the Almighty and humans are his successors and subjects within
the created order. Allah will bring the story to its conclusion. People
remain part of the story only in so far as they submit to him in all things.
Severest temporal, as well as eternal punishment, awaits those who
refuse to submit.

Adam and Eve were tempted by Satan, and they temporarily failed to
submit. Ever since that time humanity has struggled with submission
and has needed repeated reminders of their supreme duty to submit to
Allah. Allah is merciful and he has repeatedly sent prophets to remind
humanity of this responsibility. The Jewish and Christian scriptures are
a collection of the writings of some of these prophets, albeit considered
to be corrupt and unreliable. This continuing prophetic tradition is a
cornerstone within Islam.

With Mohammed came the final and corrective revelation, the perfect
recital, the seal of the prophetic. With Mohammed's political and military
successes, together with his immediate successors, came the first Islamic
Caliphate (Empire). A worldwide empire where everyone submits to
the will of Allah, to Sharia law, is the goal of the Islamic meta-story.

Sharia Law is the detailed religious legal code that governs all aspects of life within Islamic culture.

This caliphate and this alone will
bring lasting peace and tranquility to the human family. Everyone who
refuses to submit is deemed an infidel and is treated accordingly. The
natural marriage of state and religion within Islam simplifies the process
of dealing with infidels considerably. (We see more than simply a state
religion, we see a religious state.) What seems so horrific to the decadent
and narcisstic (self-centered pleasure seeking) West is a given in the

Caliphate. After all, it is the unmistakable duty of man to islam, i.e. to submit to Allah. Refusal is a crime of the highest order and is dealt with accordingly.

The theme of this meta-story is the coming of the Worldwide Caliphate. All Islam, its many sects and divisions notwithstanding, is currently anxiously awaiting the last Imam.

This last Imam is the highly anticipated Islamic Messiah, the Mahdi, the Enlightened One. This Mahdi will be more legendary than any human being that has ever appeared within the human story. This last Mahdi, from Mohammed's lineage, will engage in global Jihad, global holy war and according to Islamic eschatology (End-Times teaching), he will be eminently successful. He will subdue all resistance and set up the global Islamic caliphate, ruling from Jerusalem itself. This Mahdi will be assisted by none other than the "Jewish/Christian" Jesus. This muslim (i.e. submitting) Jesus will be successful in persuading many Jews, as well as Christians, to islam, to submit to Allah. The Mahdi, it is believed, will at long last be successful in finally bringing justice, righteousness and virtue to the global human community.

The whole world will then follow Sharia law.

> The Shia sect, based in Iran, believes in twelve Imams, all direct descendants of Mohammed. The 12th Imam did appear in the 12th century, at the zenith of Islamic culture but he disappeared. He is believed to have been taken into heaven. He will appear again to usher in the End-Times.

> All who faithfully performed Jihad, who were willing to be Allah's servants and martyrs in bringing about this worldwide caliphate, will enjoy paradise forever with all of its pure, sensuous pleasures

This passionately awaited worldwide victory will bring this meta-story to its culminating final event, the Day of Judgment. Muslims whose good deeds outweigh the bad will enter into heaven. Others, who did submit to Allah, but whose bad deeds outweigh their good deeds, will spend time in purgatory till their suffering is sufficient to make up the lack in good deeds. Those who refused to islam, to submit to Allah, will be assigned the torments of hell.

LIFE'S ULTIMATE QUESTIONS FROM ISLAM'S PERSPECTIVE

- The Question of Truth – The Foundational Question.
  - Truth is found in the Koran and the traditions of the Prophet.
  - Truth is interpreted in the community by faithful scholars.

- The Questions surrounding our Humanity.
  - The goal of life is to be a perfect successor for Allah, perfectly submissive to him.
  - Meaning is found in furthering Islamic culture and caliphate.
  - Complete and unquestioning submission to Allah is mankind's chief responsibility.

- The Question of Ethics.
  - Sharia Law provides all the guidelines for behaviour.
  - Marriage and family are to be valued. Multiple wives are allowed. Divorce is frowned upon but permitted.
  - Patriarchal Society, men are leaders at home and in the state.
  - Women are to be respected. Modesty honours the men in the family. As a help to this end, they are to remain veiled in public. (This seems to be a more recent tradition, and

is becoming increasingly Political. Early Islam seems not to have promoted the veil as much.) *A Brief History of the Veil in Islam*, www.facinghistory.org

- The Questions surrounding Evil and Suffering.
  - Humans are born with a bent towards Allah but struggle with submission.
  - Suffering is a test, a discipline, and encourages greater submission.
  - Allah is never to be questioned with respect to personal suffering. Perfect submission requires absolute acceptance.
  - Evil is caused by our human desires, the many temptations all around, and Satan's efforts to cause human kind to stumble.
  - Ultimately all evil can be traced back to Satan who competes with humanity for Allah's blessing and allegiance.

- The Questions surrounding the Future.
  - Paradise awaits all who are martyred for the cause of Allah.
  - Everyone lives only once. Resurrection and Judgment Day follow End-Time events.
  - Heaven or hell for eternity awaits all human beings.
  - Purgatory, for a time, for all Muslims whose bad deeds outweigh their good deeds.

TODAY'S GLOBAL ISLAMIC RESURGENCE
QUESTIONS FOR CONSIDERATION

1. What is fueling this Islamic Renaissance? Petroleum, Politics, Power & Pride, Western Imperialism, Islamic Jihadism and End-Times Teaching?

Life's Ultimate Questions: Exploring the Stories that Shape Our Everyday

2. Is the West's general religious illiteracy creating faulty interpretations as to what is really at issue in these conflict zones, and as a result, faulty responses politically, as well as, militarily?

3. What is at the root of why so many young people are joining militant Islamic groups? Economically disenfranchised youth, lack of education, religious vacuum within western societies (loss of meaning), the thrill of being an active participant in an Islamic End-Time scenario, something worth living for, dying for, the promise of paradise and all its sensuous pleasures if martyred?

4. Islamic populations within Europe are growing at a much faster rate than the local populations. The cultural melting pot theory does not seem to apply to their religious ghettos. How might this be interpreted in light of Islam's meta-story?

5. To what degree is the moral collapse of the West affirming a Muslim's understanding of the superior moral truth within the Koran and Sharia Law? We need to be aware that within the Islamic mindset there is no separation between religion and state. By implication, that means that the majority within Islamic cultures view Christianity as closely aligned with western culture. To what degree do Muslims view the Western World's moral collapse as the failure of Christianity? How should the church respond?

CONSIDERATIONS FROM A CHRISTIAN PERSPECTIVE

A look at Islam, and its meta-story, raises a few questions that Christianity would do well to consider.

A) Islam has indeed developed a culture that shapes the generations effectively. The five pillars provide continual faith developing practices. These are reinforced through the strength of a community that seemingly does not question its heritage. The result is a globalizing ideology that has put the whole world on edge. (Islam, within the European and North American context, is struggling to keep its young people as well but it does not seem to be to the degree that Christianity is struggling.)

Does western Christianity have a culture that effectively disciples its adherents and its next generation? For many, the obligatory one hour Sunday morning service is all that remains of a Christian community experience. Is there any intentional focus on Christian culture building, for community building, for Holy Spirit moving through body life experiences (everyone participating meaningfully)? Is Christian family culture emphasized in our homes, or has all the generational faith-shaping been delegated to the institutional church and its "one-hour" programs?

If there is any relevance to the above concerns then Christians are being shaped primarily by the prevailing culture which is predominantly materialistic and atheistic. Does this result in too many "Christians" being so in name only? Is this one of the reasons why there seems to be such a strong falling away after our young people leave home and begin life on their own? (Evangelical Fellowship of Canada's survey *"Hemorrhaging Faith"* suggests upwards of 70% leave the Christian worldview.)

Is it time for a serious conversation with a focus on the strengthening of a dynamic faith-shaping culture within church and family?

B) The Islamic traditions foster an unquestioning obedience to the Islamic worldview. Allah, the Koran, and the Prophet are beyond criticism. Any negative thought is considered blasphemy and is treated as a capital offence. Does this foster an inability to critically examine the faith-based assumptions within Islam? Does Islam and its adherents have the ability to step outside of its circular reasoning so as to self-critique its own positions. Has it developed the practice of thoughtfully providing answers to the many that are critical of its history, its religious books, or its leaders? Is this continually reinforced unquestioning temperament prone to be exploited by the Imams, Mullahs and Ayatollahs within Islam?

Christianity has been blessed throughout its long history with many outspoken critics, from state, media, as well as university. Apologists (defenders of the faith) have continually needed to go back to Christianity's foundations to reassess. They have continually needed to step outside of their circular reasoning to critically re-examine their faith assumptions. Christianity has not only survived but has thrived in this environment of intense opposition. This historical fact of criticism, and so often to the extreme, is a strong argument that should encourage anyone searching for truth to seriously consider Christianity. This faith has been tested in the fire and survived.

As suggested above, Christianity needs to continually engage in faith-shaping culture-making. This culture-making needs to include a strong emphasis on apologetics (defending the faith). Adherents need to be taken outside of the Christian culture's circular reasoning to continually reassess their faith foundations. Is Christianity losing such a large portion of its young people because they simply have not been taught how to process contemporary criticism against the faith? A Sunday School level faith understanding simply cannot stand against the power of the prevailing culture that pushes a materialistic and atheistic mind and heart-set.

C) Islam seems to have removed much of the mystery and mystic from within its experience. It seems to have replaced this with routines and rituals that can simply be followed, often without much spiritual energy.

This tendency to negate the supernatural can be seen in many Christian communities as well. At such times, Christianity is reduced to merely a set of rules and traditions to follow. It becomes simply an external subculture. Legalism, simply following and obeying rules and traditions, becomes the ingrained pattern. It is during these times that many spiritually sensitive Christians push towards a renewal of the more mystic dynamic illustrated so often within the New Testament (a relationship with Jesus, developing a sense of the presence of deity, being Spirit-led, empowered by the Spirit, listening to the Spirit, etc.).

It is one key theme of biblical teaching that a simple superficial obedience to rules and rituals spells the loss of the spiritual dynamic within the Christian life.

Between Islam and Secular Atheism – an Apology

Judaism and Christianity are the two other "revealed" religions. I have moved the Judeo-Christian story to its own section in Part 5. My original goal was to write a book where the five major religions and their meta-stories were simply to be placed side by side and then to let the reader compare and decide. That, it seems to me, will always prove to be a near impossible task since we can only think and speak (and critique) from within our own mind and heart-set. We can never really be truly neutral.

I have tried to present each of the stories constructively, presenting each with as little pre-judgment as possible. I trust I have been somewhat successful. There is something we can learn from each. Each has discovered some element of the truth. Together, they do present an overview of our human family's spiritual searching since the beginning of time.

The next meta-story, that of atheistic secularism, presents itself as the culmination of all of this human searching. It presents itself as the "finally-we-have-arrived" conclusion to all of the misguided religious searching from ages past. This next story presents itself as the "truth" that has finally eradicated all other religious stories. Is this attitude cultural pride and/or just the typical religious response? (All religions have this perspective, that they are the only truth.)

The following meta-story fails to understand that it, too, is based on assumptions that it has elevated to the status of unquestioned fact. Instead of helping to lift the fog it may simply have declared the fog normal. Its short-sightedness has simply declared that there is nothing and no one out there. We are alone!

To alleviate this fearful feeling of cosmic aloneness, has the focus shifted to one of searching for aliens living light years away? Interesting!

Secular Humanism
and its Meta-Story

Start to read at bottom left corner

• Mankind continues to evolve till he is fully in control of the wilderness within himself and in nature. Mankind becomes übermensch, Superman, Homo Evolutis.

• Mankind becomes the true HERO in the story. In our world, maybe in other galaxies too!

Atheism's story line

Theme: Progress - Evolution

• Through education we participate more fully in modernism's project – a better world through reason.

• With the help of science and technology mankind overcomes the wilderness.

• *Uneducated, unaware, ignorant, savages, technologically primitive.*

• In the Beginning Physics...
• The Big Bang
• Naturalistic materialism
• Life evolved out of the physical.

• *Too religious – controlled by fears, the unknowns, the mysteries of nature and life.*

• *Key Problem – incomplete evolution, primitive understandings and behaviours. (not sins)*

• First *Homo Sapiens appear ca. 200,000 years ago.*

Notes: The term übermensch – German philosopher Friedrich Nietzsche coined this term – the term inspired Nazi Germany's ideology of a superior race. It is translated into English as superman.

Homo evolutis (future humanoid species) – see graphic page at the end of this meta-story.

This meta-story is defined with several terms. It is **secular** because any notion of any traditional religion is irrelevant and outdated, at best a nuisance, probably even a curse on the path of progress that our planet is believed to be on. **Humanism** is central to this meta-story. Humanity has proven itself the fittest in the struggle for survival. By virtue of being the strongest, the planet 'belongs' to us. Humanity is the highest life form, the ultimate authority in the cosmos. Humanity is the hero of this story. People will eventually experience the resolution of the issues plaguing their existence. This meta-story is called **scientific** because science is the only way of knowing what is true (epistemology). Any claim, religious or otherwise, that cannot be verified by science is considered myth or erroneous. This meta-story is labeled **materialism** because the material, the physical world around us, the world of our 5 senses, is all there is. There is no spiritual dimension, no afterlife. That makes this meta-story **atheistic**. There is no god, neither one nor many. It is described as **naturalism** because nature is all there is and the source of all life. Classic evolution is embraced by this meta-story. Evolution is the embedded "guiding principle" for all of nature. All of the life forms found in nature are on a march towards ever greater complexity, towards ever greater perfection. Culturally, it is closely associated with **liberalism** because it is "Yes for most things new but out with the old." By definition most things new are progressive. This is the dominant story of our modern

> The mental climate within this worldview understands (assumes) that this worldview alone begins without any faith assumptions. It is assumed that it alone is completely based on scientifically verifiable facts. All other worldviews begin with faith assumptions. **Western culture's inability to recognize and acknowledge its own foundational faith assumptions is a critical first step that needs to be addressed.**

western culture. It may very well be your story and mine by default, if perchance we have not consciously chosen to walk another path.

Given the strength of the mental climate within the institutions of our culture it is rare that anyone stops and steps back to examine the assumptions underlying atheistic secular humanism. It is becoming more and more the case that anyone who even begins to question these underlying assumptions is summarily marginalized. As a result the few, or not so few, who disagree simply remain quiet.

Few have thought this story through to its necessary "conclusion". Evolution, according to the theory, is a continuing process. Not just mankind but all life forms are on the upward march towards "perfection". Not just the past, but the future as well, will be different than the present. All life forms will continue to either advance in their development or become extinct.

Again, even fewer have carefully considered the ethical implications that result from this worldview. Worldview, the answers to the ultimate questions, and behaviour are of necessity all inter-linked. How does the evolutionary ethical principle of survival of the fittest impact our

> Classic evolution claims that there is no God. All progress within life is simply through chance evolutionary processes. Many sincere Christians accept the evolutionary processes but include the guiding hand of God in that process. No longer simply accidental mutations but "change and progress" are now overseen by a sovereign and all powerful God. God created using evolutionary processes.
>
> Of course, atheistic evolutionary materialism categorically denies this divine presence and involvement. Theistic evolution is as far removed from classic evolution as the "no god" camp is removed from the "there is a God" camp.

sense of right and wrong? How does the evolutionary principle of accidental mutations impact humanity's search for meaning, value and purpose? How does the fact of "no god" impact our sense of justice? Justice, after all, is an appeal to an authority higher than you or I, or your tribe or my tribe.

Four Big Bangs (radical extraordinary big leaps forward) have been suggested for the planet and in particular for the human species. Possibly humanity is currently in the throws of a fifth Big Bang. Given the reality that much evolving is still needed, a sixth is suggested in order to bring humankind to its "mandated evolutionary goal."

> The first four Big Bangs have been suggested by Frank Pastore as presented online at Prager University. (The lecture, "The Four Big Bangs" available online http://vimeo.com/42378566)

FIRST BIG BANG – COSMOLOGICAL

The cosmos came to be, a something developed from nothing! The result is our ever expanding universe. This meta-story begins with, "In the beginning physics," rather than, "In the beginning God."

> Much has been made of the question as to origins. What or who caused this Big Bang? This does need an answer. But for now the important point is that this Big Bang, as well as the five that follow, all need an explanation as to what or who precipitated them! The problem is a lot more challenging than simply asking, "How did the Big Bang start?" The immediate response is, "Which one?"

SECOND BIG BANG – BIOLOGICAL

Here we find the birth of life itself and this from inanimate nonliving materials. A primordial soup spawns the first living cell: a living, growing, self-reproducing cell. All the encyclopedic information systems within this first cell's DNA molecule appears out of nothing. Not only that, but this DNA molecule's amazing self duplicating protocols that make growth and reproduction possible just start, are learned out of nothing. Absolutely amazing developments, without the guidance of any unseen hand, all happen by accident, and, by chance, moved forward only by the dynamic principles embedded in evolution.

A brief summary of basic evolutionary theory may be needed here. A select few purely **accidental genetic mutations** create advantages for some within a species. These have the tendency to survive when environmental pressures arise and they reproduce more successfully. The result is the **survival of the fittest** and the inevitable march towards ever greater complexity and perfection. Observable mini-adaptations within species and the assumed major leaps forward, have led to altogether new species. **Unimaginable time periods** are needed. The geological records and cosmological data may suggest such time periods and are interpreted as substantiating evidence. Life has developed in this way from that first living cell to the many branches of living organisms observed today.

The miracle of this first living cell is just the beginning of cosmic wonders beyond wonders. The planet that birthed this first life form must have been decidedly inhospitable to life. Any comparison to any other planet known to man confirms this truth. Some have postulated the Gaia principle which suggests a strong interplay between life and the planet. Life forms interact with the planet's atmosphere and rocky surface so that it becomes more and more habitable, more and more suitable for life to continue to evolve. Oxygen and CO_2 levels are optimized. The miracle molecule, H_2O, is released from the planet's rock stratas into the atmosphere aplenty, or it is possibly captured from some comet debris. Soil is developed and enriched. And now, billions of years later, we observe a planet that seems to have been fine-tuned in so many ways to not only make life possible, but to make life flourish in an abundance of diversity and beauty and plenty. All by accident, by chance! The fact that life and the life supporting biosphere exist today is evidence enough, according to this meta-story, that it indeed happened in this way, so many eons ago.

Physics today continues to refine the laws of thermodynamics (no longer mere theories but so certain as to declare them to be laws). These laws dictate that everything on planet Earth (or the closed system of the cosmos) is increasing in randomness, tending towards increased disorder (Entropy). This downward direction is an absolute certainty for everything. That would be the end of the story if it were not for evolution and its principle of progress and ever increasing orderliness or complexity. Life with its embedded theory of evolution has more-often-than-not trumped the laws of thermodynamics. Thank "god" it has, and so life has blossomed on this "miraculous one-of-a-kind" planet.

There is indeed the one in a trillion-million possibility that randomness would result in the complexity of the simplest DNA molecule. It does indeed take a lot of faith to believe that this has happened so consistently to make all the beauty and diversity happen that is so obviously observable today.

Sooner or later science will, with the greatest of certainty, discover another planet somewhere, possibly millions of light years away, where life has developed just as it has here on planet earth. That will be confirmation beyond a doubt that evolution (without a God) indeed happened on our planet. For now just the discovery of the miracle molecule, water, on Mars, by the Mars Rover or its sister Curiosity, is sufficient proof that it indeed must have been so!

THIRD BIG BANG - ANTHROPOLOGICAL

Evolution's greatest "achievement" is humanity! Even just a cursory comparison with animals suggests something very unique has happened to the human DNA molecule. Physically, the human body operates with essentially the same chemistry and biology as all animals do, even as the simplest one-celled organism does. Yet, intuitively, we all realize that humans are somehow unique. Humans do not only operate on a significantly higher level intellectually; they operate on a different paradigm. A different "operating system" has been embedded within humans. Plants respond to light, animals are programmed to respond to instinct, humans use rational choices to direct their actions. Our ability to reason, to consider consequences and alternatives, to make decisions consciously based on evidence carefully gathered, sometimes over time, by our 5 senses, sets us on a different trajectory when compared to animals.

Evolutionary biologists, whose task it is to uncover the processes that illustrate evolution, are able to point to many animal behaviours that suggest that the generic DNA molecule has been pre-programmed to develop these unique abilities that we now observe in humans. As an example, people develop language skills at an early age. The great apes have been taught, using much time and patience and skill, to say simple words as well. Clear evidence, it is assumed, that shows that language has been "pre-programmed" into life's generic DNA pool. Another example is the amazing ability of people to invent tools and improve technology from generation to generation. Here too, rudimentary tool use is seen in some animals. Otters use stones to break open clams. Monkeys have been observed using sticks to pry open fruit. Clear evidence, it is assumed, that the generic DNA molecule is pre-disposed to the development of tools as well. If we accept evolutionary theory we can safely deduce that pre-monkeys, 200 000 years ago ((the time when the first biped humanoid appeared) did not use sticks. Their DNA has helped them evolve to a higher level as well. And ancient otters could not possibly have known about rocks and clams.

What more can be said about humankind's amazing interest, creativity and skill in the fields of architecture, clothing, agriculture, weaponry, music, art, and literature to name just a few. Amazing evolutionary development to be sure! But with careful research, similar growth can be seen in the animal world. It is safe to assume, then, that pre-beavers did not build such elaborate lodges and dams as they do now. Neither did pre-bees build such complex hives. To be sure, pre-hyenas would not have had such skillful group hunting practices as they display today. The DNA molecule is pre-programmed to push all creatures forward. It is just that humans have experienced this third Big Bang; the anthropological giant leap forward that has set them apart from other life forms in all areas culturally and intellectually.

When looking at the human species physically in comparison

As an aside, if one accepts evolutionary development theory, one must also count on evolution to continue to be at work in the animal world. It may be sooner than we think that we will have as pets, "dogs" that not only listen to our every command, but ones that talk back as well! We may also enjoy "monkeys" that have developed greater intellectual capacity so as to perform some of our more mundane tasks. Who knows, we may even have pets that have become perfect bipeds as us! And "lions" may have evolved enough to tame their violent streaks and become condo companions for the lonely, the weak or the more adventurous among us.

to other animals one must wonder what has happened to all the physical advantages that the humanoid ancestors must have had in order to succeed in the battle of the "survival of the fittest" prior to this Big Bang – the anthropological. Physically, humans are at the mercy of most animals. We can easily find a predatory animal or two that is faster, or more adept at fighting (our fingernails versus the claws of a tiger), others see better, run faster, have stronger teeth, and all keep themselves warm more easily. We could go on and on. Humans must have had some superior physical abilities prior to their intellectual ascendancy. They would never have survived otherwise. What has happened to these advantages? Have they been lost through non-use? How might that have happened using evolutionary processes as an explanation? The only physical advantage that we seem to have is an advanced opposable thumb which makes the holding of tools possible.

FOURTH BIG BANG – PSYCHOLOGICAL

The evidence for this giant leap forward is found in the human psyche. Humans seem to experience life to a much deeper level than any of our animal counterparts.

Humans struggle with issues of good and evil, with right and wrong. Humans "instinctively" know that "survival of the fittest" within the human family is so very, very inhumane. We all judge others in terms of how gently they treat the weakest. A culture's treatment of women, of children, of the elderly, of the dying, even the treatment of animals becomes the standard for evaluating that culture. A paradigm shift has occurred that sets humankind a world apart from animals where survival of the fittest does indeed reign supreme.

Humans struggle to know truth and meaning. Philosophy (with its sub-branch religion) (or the reverse, religion with its sub-branch philosophy) has been humanity's most enduring intellectual enterprise. The loss of meaning has resulted in more suicides than most other crises humans face. The suicide pandemic among young people in western societies today suggests that inner emptiness in terms of meaning, the seeming pointlessness of life, needs to be satisfied if one is to survive. Humans long to feel significant. They long to make a difference. They long to leave the world a better place when they pass on. They dream of leaving a legacy for generations to come. If this eludes the individual, what becomes of him or her?

Evolution is all about survival. Survival is, as someone has coined, all about "getting food, getting by, and getting laid." Yet here we find humans desperately searching for values that have nothing to do with mere survival. Humans are not merely part of the struggle for survival but also seem to be participants in what some have called a sacred dance.

Humans struggle for deeper relationships, a sense of belonging, a community of unconditional acceptance. They struggle for justice. Humans struggle with fear, the fear of being excluded, the fear of meaninglessness. They have a built-in longing for continuing life even up to their dying breath. They long for a place and a time where deepest dreams do indeed come true.

FIFTH BIG BANG – BIO-TECHNOLOGICAL

Humans may very well be in the midst of another Big Bang. With the advent of advanced technological expertise, especially nanotechnology and biotechnology, humans are increasingly playing an active role in their own destiny. Gene splicing, cloning, and DNA nano-surgery are making humans partners in the evolutionary process. Never before, in the long history of evolution, has there been a time when a species begins to play a significant part in its own march towards perfection. According to this meta-story that may very well be happening now!

Atheism's meta-story can already envision an era when common diseases, common genetic defects and perceived negative human traits may become obsolete because of science sponsored and/or evolutionary DNA breakthroughs. In the meantime, traditional medicine has been able to control everything from depression to anger outbursts. Once greed has been successfully defined as a negative and destructive trait, then medicine, too, will be able to control it. There will be a pill, a patch, or a needle for most anything until such a time that bio-techno-nano-nuclear medicine, together with evolution, eliminates the problem permanently!

Our cultural stress on education, especially in the sciences, is consistent with this perspective. The more educated we become, the better we will be able to participate positively with the forces embedded in evolution. No longer will it be just accidental improvements but now **intelligent design at the behest of humanity itself**! The perfect society, postulated and illustrated so well by the immensely popular Star Trek Enterprise TV series or the superman and superwoman genre, is now within reach. And, who can visualize what comes after that!

SIXTH BIG BANG – DEIFICATION

If per chance planet earth is destroyed before humanity has self-perfected itself, no need to worry, new livable planets will have been discovered where humankind can continue on its evolutionary journey. Perhaps even, and with this we speculate, other highly evolved life forms that humanity has discovered will be suitable for mating purposes (DNA science will have made that possible) and human evolution could very well receive a significant jump forward – the sixth Big Bang.

But one thing is sure, the progressive forces inherent in evolution will "guarantee" an ever onward, ever upward march towards perfection and to ever more elevated paradigms of existence until "neo-humans" can rightly assume, with dignity and deservedly, the title of "gods and goddesses" of the universe.

Neo-human: a term from "Neo-Humanity 2045: A Global Strategy for the Evolution of Humanity in the Third Millennium" http://2045.com/articles/29103.html

But before we celebrate (there is always the "but"), these futuristic scenarios of course apply only to the "human" DNA molecule and the humanoid life-form that will then be used as its host. You and I will long have ceased to exist, having served our purpose merely by successfully passing our DNA on to the next generation. But then (another but!), that compliment would only apply to us if perchance we were part of that select group of humans with advanced genes, humans with nobility or celebrity status in some domain of excellence. The rest of us are simply the million non-essentials, essential only in creating the random context for the "one in a million" that actually does move the human DNA molecule forward.

<u>**BUT THEN AGAIN – WHAT IF ...**</u>

> And if, perchance, the pessimism of our culture destroys all faith for such a positive "ending" for the human story, there is no need to lose faith in the evolutionary processes. (The glory due to this amazing power embedded in nature must forever remain undiminished!)

> It may indeed turn out that the human species is not destined for such lofty evolutionary development. There is indeed no prophesy embedded within the accidental processes of evolution. If, perchance, the evolution of the human species is unsustainable, and if, perchance, the species has indeed become too "advanced" for its own good, then extinction may very well be in the cards. If, perchance, the species has developed technological prowess (e.g. know-how to make H Bombs) without moral improvement, and is indeed destined to self-destruct before it morally self-perfects, then evolution will not even blink an eye, will not even consider whether it had made an error. The power embedded within

evolution is without personality, has no need to consider or reconsider or find fault or self correct.

Another species will simply fill the "void" left by human-kind; will become the destiny-blessed survivor for the next round at the roulette table of life. And humankind's longing for justice, for love, for meaning, purpose and legacy will turn out to have been merely a self-imposed narcissistic dream possibly caused by faulty chemical interactions – no doubt caused by the tragic and unnecessary detour called "religion".

But then who will care and would it even matter?

LIFE'S ULTIMATE QUESTIONS FROM ATHEISM'S PERSPECTIVE

- The Question of Truth — The Foundational Question.
  - Science is the measure of all truth. If science cannot prove it, then it is a myth.
  - No god, no spiritual dimension. Matter is all there is.

- The Questions Surrounding our Humanity.
  - Humans are highly evolved animals.
  - Life has no inherent meaning. Every individual human being needs to create his/her own meaning for life's short journey (e.g. adventure, family, career, sex, my country, my team, my celebrity, etc.).

- The Question of Ethics.
  - ◻ Moral truth is relative, to each his own, no absolutes. (Note – the only absolute truth is, "There is no absolute truth. Everything is in flux. Evolution means change.")
  - ◻ To each his/her own brand of sexuality as long as no one gets hurt. Marriage is evolving; it is as you define it. And now it seems that even our gender is subject to choice.
  - ◻ Biologically, sex is just about procreation, but if humankind can find more uses for it, then why not give it a try.
  - ◻ Our higher values (e.g. do not hurt others) are the result of evolved social consensus. This evolved social consensus must live in tension with evolution's ongoing principle, survival of the fittest.

- The Questions Surrounding Evil and Suffering.
  - ◻ Evolution is, as yet, unfinished. Perfection awaits in the future.
  - ◻ Too many people are not getting with the program, too many are religiously holding on to old-fashioned ideas like God and religious ideologies.

- The Questions Surrounding the Future.
  - ◻ Death is the end. We die just as the animals do. Complete your bucket list because that's it!
  - ◻ No Judgment Day for me, none for Hitler or Stalin either.
  - ◻ Some future humanoid species will enjoy a much better ride on their journeys across the planet's stage (that is, if humans have not gone extinct or if the planet is still inhabitable).

ebook advertised on Kindle, February. 2013
(used with permission)

Book Abstract

There have been at least 25 prototype humans. We are but one more model, and there is no evidence evolution has stopped. So unless you think Rush Limbaugh and Howard Stern are the be all and end all of creation, and it just does not get any better, then one has to ask what is next? Juan Enriquez and Steve Gullans, two of the world's most eminent science authors, researchers, and entrepreneurs, answer this by taking you into a world where humans increasingly shape their environment, their own selves, and other species. It is a world where our bodies harbor 100 times more microbial cells than human cells, a place where a gene cocktail may allow many more to climb an 8,000 meter peak without oxygen, and where, given the right drug, one could have a 77 percent chance of becoming a centenarian. By the end you will see a broad, and sometimes scary, map of life science driven change. Not just our bodies will be altered but our core religious, government, and social structures as humankind makes the transition to a new species, a Homo evolutis, which directly and deliberately controls its own evolution and that of many other species.

Atheism's Trinity

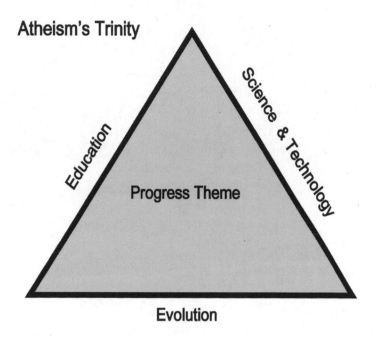

Science & Technology

Education

Progress Theme

Evolution

Atheism's Keys to a Better World!

200 000 years from today

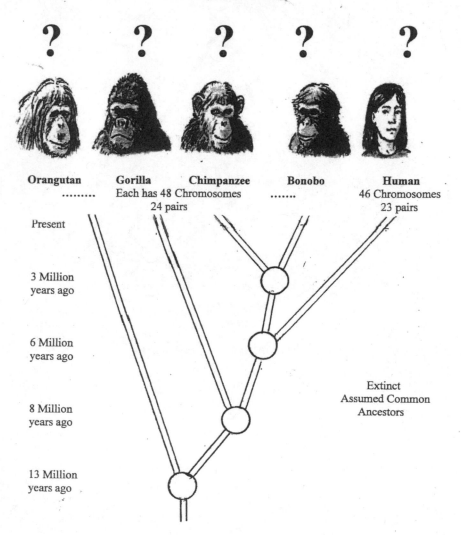

Adapted from http://www.angelfire.com/cellophanetales/evolution.html

151

Places to Worship the Pride of Humanity.
The Mall, the Stadium, the Silver and Digital Screen.

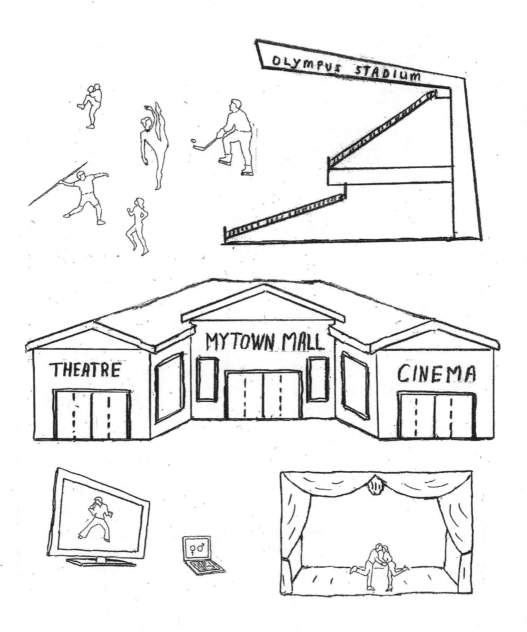

Life's Ultimate Questions: Exploring the Stories that Shape Our Everyday

Plato, Moses, and Aristotle

THE THREE GREAT MINDS OF WESTERN CIVILIZATION
Plato was a 4th century BCE philosopher during the zenith of the Greek Empire (Alexander the Great, 356 to 323 BCE, founder of the Empire). The emphasis of Plato's thinking stressed the realities of the invisible world, if you like the spiritual world. The physical was less real, less ideal. The physical existed more in the mind, appeared real only by way of our five senses. By way of example, our true humanity was to be found in the invisible soul. The soul was trapped inside the physical body and needed to be set free from this prison to really prosper. The invisible world, the spiritual dimension was primary.

Aristotle was Plato's student. He begged to differ with his teacher. For him, reality was found more in the physical world. The spiritual dimension, the invisible, existed in the mind and was an extension of the mind. The physical world was very real, was good and worthy of respect.

Moses (1400 BCE) was the founder of Hebrew culture and the Judeo-Christian worldview. His foundational premise was that both the physical, as well as the spiritual worlds, were very real. The spiritual was foundational and supportive of the physical. The spiritual created and supported the real physical world. The Bible begins with, "In the beginning God created the world" and it ends, "He will make all things, i.e. heaven and earth, new." Not one or the other, both are very real and will remain real into eternity.

Christianity, early in its development, drifted from its Hebraic roots, and embraced a more Platonic worldview. This thinking gave birth to the hermit lifestyle and the monastic traditions, both of which shunned the material world. Saint Augustine of Hippo (354 – 430 CE) was one of its chief spokesmen.

The European church (and culture with it) shifted towards Aristotle during the 13th Century. Thomas Aquinas (1225 – 1274 CE) was instrumental in moving the church and culture towards this philosophical tradition.

Did the prevailing anti-Semitism contribute to the church's and culture's failure to clearly embrace the middle road, the Mosaic worldview?

The Aristotelian worldview, with its emphasis on physical reality, gave birth to science and its phenomenal successes. The church's emphasis on the teaching that an all-wise God created a good and ordered world, encouraged study in the natural sciences. Many early scientists were devout Christians. Their discoveries within the realm of science encouraged their faith. They saw so much evidence for a Designer Creator God in the facts being uncovered by science. But over the centuries scienticism (the marriage between atheism and science) has killed its parent, Christianity.

These three traditions, and their struggle for supremacy, have formed the intellectual foundation for all of western culture. Today we live in an Aristotelian worldview to the extreme – the spiritual has been fully eclipsed by the physical.

Today we live during a time of great cultural stress. Many are rethinking the very foundations of our culture. Have we as a culture arrived at a point where we are beginning to realize that our very survival is in doubt because of the excesses and extremes of a "this-world-only" perspective? (Is spirituality i.e. Plato, coming back?)

PLATO, MOSES, AND ARISTOTLE SIDE BY SIDE

The next several pages need to be read comparatively as a 3 page centerfold. (Spare your eyes. These columns are presented on the following pages in full size print.)

Plato, Moses, Aristotle Side by Side	and the Three Philosophical / Religious Traditions	for the Average You and Me.
Plato	**Moses**	**Aristotle**
First Principle Ultimate Reality is to be found in the spiritual, in the mind.	**First Principle** Ultimate Reality is found in both. The physical world is created and sustained by the Spiritual.	**First Principle** Reality is best found in the physical world of our senses.
The things that fill the physical world of our senses are ultimately only projections from our mind.	It is not either / or but both! Both need to be embraced as good and as real.	The spiritual world is separate from the physical world and is real only in so far as it is supported by our mind.
The physical world is real only in so far, as it is supported by the mind, the imagination, the spirit.		
First Principle developed to its logical conclusion Developing this foundational first principle to its logical conclusion we find the mindset of eastern religions.	**First Principle developed to its logical conclusion** Developing this foundational first principle to its logical conclusion we find the heart set that embraces the world as a beautiful gift from the loving God – the Hebrew tradition.	**First Principle developed to its logical conclusion** Developing this foundational first principle to its logical conclusion we find the mindset of atheistic materialism, the spiritual has been completely marginalized; God has been "killed."
In Hinduism and Buddhism we read that all that is physical and material is an illusion. We read that ultimate reality is to be found only in the Ultimate Spiritual Unity principle.	In the Judeo – Christian tradition we understand that human sin has caused a separation between God and man, between the spiritual and the physical. This separation is the cause of all the suffering and the chaos on planet earth. The spiritual no longer sustains the physical.	In the western world of humanism and consumerism we read that God and all things spiritual are an illusion. Ultimate reality is found only in the physical elements and the scientific laws that govern them.
Human Redemption As a result redemption is to be found in becoming One (e.g. Nirvana) with the Unifying Spirit of the World – call this Oneness what you like: Brahman, Buddha, the Ground of all being, the Light, the Ocean of Tranquility, God etc.	**Human Redemption** As a result redemption is found in healing the rift between the spiritual and the physical, between God and humankind, and allowing them to become reconciled again. The Kingdom of God, his Spirit fully sustaining the physical, will have been completely restored, will again display perfect unity, perfect Oneness, perfect shalom. (Both will be: a new heaven and a new earth, not one or the other)	**Human Redemption** As a result "redemption" is to be found in enjoying life to the extreme, going out with a bang, and then becoming one with the elements that constituted the body to begin with. The "soul, if there is one" ceases with the body.
Process of Redemption The process of redemption involves the cleansing of the "self" from all the illusionary desires for the things of this world. This happens through many, many life times of suffering until the "self" learns that desire for the illusionary things of this world is what destroys.	**Process of Redemption** Redemption involves the cleansing of the cosmos and the human heart from all the sin and evil that has destroyed the unity between God and humankind. This salvation is found in Jesus, in the mystery of his cross and resurrection.	**Process of Redemption** The process of redemption involves the cleansing of the "self" from all the illusionary religious principles that restrict the desires for, and the enjoyment of the things of this world.
This Mindset is illustrated best by the wandering Hindu ascetic or the smiling meditative Buddha or early Christianity's hermit and monastic culture that had renounced all material enjoyments to simply spend time in prayer and contemplation. (Christianity embraced much platonic philosophy in its early growth within the Greco – Roman world.)	**This Mindset is illustrated best** by the mystery incarnation of Jesus (God in human form). Jesus, living as a perfect human being, fully enlightened and empowered by the Spirit of God, and as a result living in perfect harmony and dependence on the spiritual dimension.	**This Mindset is illustrated best** by the empty shell of so much celebrity culture, a culture that has everything physical that it could possibly desire but in the process has bankrupted its inner soul.
	Further to this, all humans are called to follow Jesus, confessing their sin, submitting to the Spirit of God who again indwells every disciple. They begin the process of learning to depend on this Holy Spirit to live in harmony with Ultimate Reality –	This mindset, by extension, is further illustrated by us all when we worship at the altar of celebrity culture, an obsessive 20th – 21st century pastime.

PLATO

First Principle
Ultimate Reality is to be found in the spiritual, in the mind.
The things that fill the physical world of our senses are ultimately
   only projections from our mind.
The physical world is real only in so far as it is supported by the
   mind, the imagination and the spirit.

First Principle developed to its logical conclusion
Developing this foundational first principle to its logical conclusion
   we find the mindset of eastern religions.
In Hinduism and Buddhism we read that all that is physical and
   material is an illusion. We read that ultimate reality is to be
   found only in the Ultimate Spiritual Unity principle.

Human Redemption
As a result of this first principle, redemption is to be found in
   becoming One (e.g. nirvana) with the Unifying Spirit of the
   World — call this Oneness what you like: Brahman, Buddha,
   the Ground of all being, the Light, the Ocean of Tranquility,
   God, etc.

Process of Redemption
The process of redemption involves the cleansing of the "self"
   from all the illusionary desires for the things of this world. This
   happens through many, many life times of suffering until the
   "self" learns that desire for the illusionary things of this world is
   what destroys.

This Mindset is illustrated best by the wandering Hindu ascetic or
   the smiling meditative Buddha or early Christianity's hermit and
   monastic culture that had renounced all material enjoyments to
   simply spend time in prayer and contemplation. (Christianity

embraced much Platonic philosophy in its early growth within the Greco-Roman world.)

MOSES

First Principle
Ultimate Reality is found in both; the physical world is created and sustained by the spiritual. It is not either/or but both! Both need to be embraced as good and as real.

First Principle developed to its logical conclusion
Developing this foundational first principle to its logical conclusion we find the heart-set that embraces the world as a beautiful gift from the loving God – the Hebrew tradition.

In the Judeo-Christian tradition we understand that human sin has caused a separation between God and man, between the spiritual and the physical. This separation is the cause of all the suffering and the chaos on planet earth. The spiritual no longer sustains the physical.

Human Redemption
As a result, redemption is found in healing the rift between the spiritual and the physical, between God and humankind, and allowing them to become reconciled again. The Kingdom of God, his Spirit fully sustaining the physical, will have been completely restored, will again display perfect unity, perfect Oneness, perfect shalom. Both will be, a new heaven and a new earth, not one or the other.

Process of Redemption
Redemption involves the cleansing of the cosmos and the human heart from all the sin and evil that has destroyed the unity

between God and humankind. This salvation is found in Jesus, in the mystery of his cross and resurrection.

This Mindset is illustrated best by the mystery of the incarnation of Jesus (God in human form). Jesus, fully enlightened and empowered by the Spirit of God, lived as a perfect human being in dependence on the spiritual dimension.
Further to this, all of humanity is called to follow Jesus, confessing their sin, submitting to the Spirit of God who again indwells every disciple. They begin the process of learning to depend on this Holy Spirit to live in harmony with Ultimate Reality – God.

(This "living like Jesus" dynamic will be presented in more detail in the Judeo-Christian meta-story.)

ARISTOTLE

First Principle
Reality is best found in the physical world of our senses.
The spiritual world is separate from the physical world and is real only in so far as it is supported by our mind.

First Principle developed to its logical conclusion
Developing this foundational first principle to its logical conclusion we find the mindset of atheistic materialism, the spiritual, has been completely marginalized; God has been "killed".
In the western world of humanism and materialism, we read that God and all things spiritual are an illusion. Ultimate reality is

found only in the physical elements and the scientific laws that govern them.

Human Redemption

As a result, redemption is to be found in enjoying life to the extreme, going out with a bang, and then becoming one with the elements with which the body began. The soul, if there is one, ceases with the body.

Process of Redemption

The process of redemption involves the cleansing of the "self" from all the illusionary religious principles that restrict the desires for, and the enjoyment of, the things of this world.

This Mindset is illustrated best by the empty shell of so much celebrity culture, a culture that has everything physical that it could possibly desire but in the process has bankrupted its soul.

This mindset, by extension, is further illustrated by us all when we worship at the altar of celebrity culture, an obsessive 20th — 21st century pastime.

PATHWAY TO CONFIDENCE

1. Empowering Spirituality

2. Cultural Awareness

3. Religious Literacy

4. *Validating our Faith Assumptions*

5. Encountering the Kingdom Story

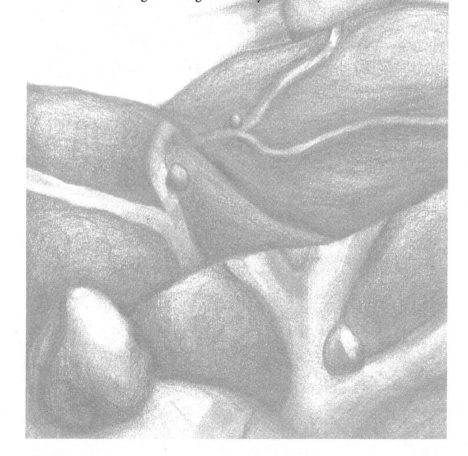

Part 4: Validating our Faith Assumptions

a few thoughts to begin with...

The thesis of this book is that it is important for us to discover and examine the faith foundations of our lives. It is important to realize that everyone, including atheists, have faith assumptions that underpin their whole belief system. This belief system is rooted in the cosmic story in which we see ourselves as participants. These assumptions together form the worldview or the religion that undergirds our whole lives. A careful analysis of personal faith assumptions is important because the resulting belief system determines all of our behavioural choices, and these, in turn, shape our destiny.

Many go through life without ever really stopping to dig deep for validation of one's personal framework for life. This failure does not bode well for depth of character. It may be a good, even necessary thing, when a life crisis forces us to pause and examine "our truth" assumptions.

No one wants to wear the label "brainwashed". This happens when a person has made but is unaware of foundational assumptions, or has subconsciously elevated faith assumptions to the category of verifiable fact.

The Challenge of Circular Reasoning

Circular reasoning is a fact of life. It is a practice that is central to all of our lives. It isn't wrong in the day to day living of our lives. It is problematic when we use it to argue the validity of a truth claim. Circular reasoning becomes a danger when we do not recognize it in our lives. It becomes a trap when we never step outside of that circle to critically question the initial assumptions.

Circular reasoning, sometimes called begging the question, or vicious circle, happens when we use our initial assumption somewhere in the argument to prove that same assumption (usually reworded) with one or more steps in between.

> Paul: "God must exist."
> Peter: "How do you know?"
> Paul: "I know because the Bible says so!"
> Peter: "How do you know the Bible is true?"
> Paul: "Because God wrote it!"

CHRISTIANS AND CIRCULAR REASONING
People of the Christian faith assume God exists, and as a consequence, see God everywhere. Every "sighting" strengthens the conviction that God indeed does exist. They give thanks to God for the beauty all around as well as the food on their dinner plate. They pray to him for guidance

and help and for more faith to believe when he seems distant or his ways are impossible to understand.

If believers would always need to go back to their foundational assumption "God is" and establish proof they would never be able to get on with the business of living. But now and again it is absolutely necessary to step outside the circular reasoning to discern the reliability of that foundational assumption, "There is a God".

Christians naturally point to the Bible for ultimate proof because their answer to "What is truth?" is that truth has been revealed to us in the Bible. This causes the circular reasoning dilemma above.

ATHEISTS AND CIRCULAR REASONING

The same is true for atheists who assume that God does not exist. As a consequence, they look around and see no evidence for God. Stuff happens and they say it is a direct consequence of some previous action or fate or chance or luck because, obviously, there is no God. There is something, there is life, rather than nothing in this cosmos. They assume it is there because of physics, biology, chemistry; it could not be God, obviously, because there is no God. These atheists too, would need to every now and again step outside of this cycle of circular reasoning to discern the reliability of their foundational assumption, "There is no God".

Atheists would naturally point to science to prove that God does not exist. For atheists, the answer to "What is truth?" is that science is the measure of all truth. Science cannot prove God and therefore it is logically assumed there is no God. Now we have developed another circular reasoning argument.

Petra: "Is there a God?"
Paula: "No, there is no God, because science, using the scientific method, cannot find any evidence for God!"
Petra: "How do you know that is true?"

Paula: "It is true, because in principle, all truth is established by reason working through science and the scientific method."

We as humans can never fully step outside of our circular reasoning when it comes to first principles. We inevitably come back to these same first principles or axioms, i.e. assumptions, which must be accepted as a faith precept. These precepts cannot be proved.

"Some philosophies state that we can never escape circular reasoning because the arguments always come back to axioms or first principles." Quoted from *Logically Fallacious* by Bo Bennett, (www - *Circular reasoning* / Bo Bennett)

Some First Principles (Axioms)
To help us in our discussion let's list some axioms. All the answers to the key Ultimate Life question, "What is Truth?" are axioms.
Some examples:

There is a God; There are many gods; There is no god.
Truth about God is found in the Bible;
Truth about Allah is found in the Koran;
Truth is found in reason working through science;
Truth is found in the Buddhist story line;
There is no absolute truth, all truth is relative.

These first principles and others like them, must be accepted by faith. Therefore, by definition, they are all religious in nature. They cannot be proven logically because that invariably involves circular reasoning.

To be sure, many philosophical arguments have been developed to help support one's adopted first principle. But experience has shown these arguments really only convince the already convinced. Part of this dilemma is caused by the fact that all of these arguments are focused on the mind, but the avenue to "our truth" is first of all through the heart.

What we love determines what we believe, and how we argue; rarely is it the other way around.

If we want there to be a god, then our mind will develop umpteen arguments to prove that truth principle. If we want there to be no god, then we will develop just as many arguments that prove that first principle. In each case, our set of arguments will just seem so absolutely convincing! We fail to realize that we have simply proven our many loves! The mind serves the heart, rather than the other way around.

A Short History of the First Principle / the Axiom for "What is Truth?"

Prior to the classical age of the Greek philosophers (Socrates, Plato, and Aristotle), **the gods and the myths surrounding them** established the patterns for what was true.

The Greek philosophers (ca. 400 BCE) challenged the gods and established **reason as the foundation for truth**.

During the great Roman Empire it was **Might is Right** (ca. 100 BCE — 300 CE). It was the mighty Roman armies that enforced their version of the truth.

Christianity stormed the bastions of Roman idolatry. Many felt it did compromise too much with Greek and Roman philosophy. The great age of compromise (ca 300 – 1400 CE) lasted till the Renaissance era. The church, wed to the state as it was, was continually challenged to remain true to its roots. However, the church's influence over culture was strong enough that culture officially adopted the worldview that was revealed in the Bible. The Western World's first principle became **revealed truth, i.e. the Bible, is the pathway to truth**. All too often, Bible truths were interpreted to fit one's own way of thinking. Compromise continued. Growing pockets of true Christianity, however, did continue to grow wherever the Bible was allowed to shape life.

The modern age began with Descarte, 16th century — when he famously said, "I think, therefore I am." **Reason, it was now assumed, was the foundation of all truth.** (Science is reason in action through the logic of the scientific method.) Reason was "reborn", the Renaissance era flourished, Plato and, even more so Aristotle were back!

Post-modernism (ca. 1960's – today) began when it was discovered, maybe better said, when we finally admitted that all of our thinking is subject to the thinker's personal perspective. No one is perfectly neutral and as a result, perfectly logical. As a result, today's first principle is **Truth is relative, everyone creates his/her own truth.**

What will tomorrow's first principle be? It may very well be logical to think that it is becoming **Might is Right** again. In many situations (e.g. business and foreign affairs) this is practically the case already. It all too often seems that in civilian conflict situations the one who can afford the best lawyer(s) wins the case!

Our global community has forced us to ask, "How do eastern cultures answer the question regarding truth?" That adds even more possibilities. That makes our human dilemma with respect to truth even more complicated. The contemporary mindset, today's first principle, is further reinforced to simply say, **"To each his own; I have mine, you have yours; truth is relative, there are no absolutes."**

It has often been observed that history repeats itself. After a time of cultural and global chaos that is being created by the last mentioned first principle, it may seem more than reasonable that many would again turn to deity. For many it may seem more than logical to believe that man does indeed need a revelation from God himself (or from the gods) if he is ever to get a handle on the questions that are so important for life and civilization.

Evolution is really the wrong word for that last statement. Evolution has within it the idea that we are making progress, but obviously, we are just going in circles.

The above was just a short overview of the evolution of the first principle with respect to "What is truth?" within our global community.

If we are really honest with ourselves as a collective human family, we should recognize that last mentioned mindset as a "We are lost!"

confession. What prevents us from admitting that? The Bible would suggest that it is human pride, an "I'll do it my way" thinking. As a result, the Bible continues by stating that pride is our greatest sin.

In response to our "being lost" dilemma, we can throw up our hands in despair. We can hide our heads in the sand. We can bury our anxiety in a bottle. We can numb our fears with any number of drugs. We can distract ourselves with any amount of meaningless entertainment. We can encourage our governments to build our armies second to none so that at least our "truth" will be respected. Or, we can admit that there really is a much greater reality out there that we as humans cannot discern with our finite minds. We are indeed knocking on the knowledge-ceiling that leads to the mystery, the wonder of what it really means to be human.

We need to continue our journey into this last frontier but the focus needs to be more on the

There is much in creation that illustrates our profound human finiteness. Physically we are so vulnerable to so much that is beyond our control. Yes, we can change the colour of our hair (temporarily). We can change our body image (for a short term, if we are hyper disciplined). We can improve our health crisis (for a short duration). We are even able to determine the day and hour of our death. And just now, in the news, our gender is subject to choice as well! All of these give us the illusion of being in control. If, however, we would but stop and think we would quickly realize that we are so very limited in all that really matters. All of the above are really only struggles with the unchangeable realities of our lives. If we are so limited physically, it is reasonable to conclude that we are limited intellectually as well, and even more so spiritually.

human heart, because the mind is stuck, trapped, blocked, in short, lost. We need to stop and listen to the whisperings of our heart. The mystics would all suggest, "Contemplate, meditate, listen for the Mystery." Many who have personally walked this road would quietly say, "He is there and he is not silent, listen for the still small voice."

The Bible would simply suggest,
"Be still and know that I am God."
Psalm 46:10

Maybe this is a good place to prayerfully press the "**pause**" button for a season. Logical argument may be able to move the mind. **More is needed to move the heart.**

Reality Checks for Scientific, Historical, and Experiential Truths

What follows here are just a few basic strategies that can help the weary traveller find a pathway to truth. We suggest four kinds of knowledge, four layers of truth: scientific, historical, experiential, and religious. **The greater the alignment between these four layers, the greater the assurance of being on the path towards truth**. Ultimate proof is not possible; we are dealing with axioms. The best we can hope for, intellectually, is reasonableness.

To begin with, how does each of these layers do reality checks so as to minimize the circular reasoning trap, the personal bias blind spot?

Science does reality checks through the scientific method which insists that observations must be made in the context of the lab, whether in a test tube or the laboratory of life or the laboratory of the universe. These observations must be repeatable by other scientists in other

Another one of our culture's huge errors is that it has elevated the science truth so high as to essentially minimize, if not negate, the others. Each of the truth layers has strengths, each has limitations. Together they provide a limited understanding of our place within the human and the cosmic story.

contexts. In this way science has been very successful in establishing truth-facts within the physical material world. Science truth-facts so established are one layer of truth.

The earth is at the perfect distance from the sun, the earth's atmosphere is at exactly the right composition, the 4 forces within the universe (gravity, electromagnetic, weak radioactive decay, and strong nuclear) are each exactly at the right strength to make the cosmos, and life possible.

But sometimes these truth-facts established by science need to be interpreted and these interpretations invariably involve one's personal perspective; one's personally adopted first principle. As an example, science has uncovered many examples of an amazing fine-tuning in astronomy, physics, chemistry, and biology.

150 of such fine-tuning facts have been uncovered. (See "Famous Quotes" in Stone #8 for comment and reference.) To explain this delicate fine-tuning, you need a first principle. Is it God? Is it accident or chance? Is it just physics? Or is it God who is, among other things, physics or at least the creator of physics, as well?

History is another layer of truth. Not lab work and experimentation but historical documents, the more original the better, and archaeological artifacts establish historical truths. History invariably gets rewritten every generation. Perspectives have changed. More facts are uncovered. Hence the interpretations may also need adjustments; maybe even completely new interpretations are presented. History does reality checks when historians over several generations collectively re-examine the historical evidence and re-examine the interpretations that have been given. Many different eyes and many different perspectives, and slowly, we do get closer to the truth. This is another layer of truth.

Human experiences are yet another layer of truth. Reality checks are done by collecting and analyzing people's experiences. (The larger the population sample the more reliable the results.) The more people's experiences are similar, the more truthfulness is assumed. If only one person has a type of experience, we might say that s/he is deluded, insane, or the reverse, an eccentric, possibly a genius, ahead of his/ her time. If many people have that same experience then it becomes "normal, true" by definition.

> Is this the rationale for all the hype within the LGBT community today, (lesbian, gay, bisexual, transgender)? The more people that share this lifestyle, that go public, the more "normal, i.e. true" these experiences become.
>
> Modernism's over-riding theme of "progress" suggests that change may very well be positive. The "good" is evolving. How might this shape a study on human experiences that has as a goal, establishing "normal"? (But then it may not be politically correct to even speak of "normal" today.)

Categories that depend heavily on this truth layer are the paranormal or the supernatural, spiritual / religious experiences, and metaphysical or the ethereal, i.e. otherworldly. A few reflections on these experiences and the challenge as to how to validate them…

- It is hard to argue against experiences especially when more and more people are reporting them.
- These experiences, by definition, are outside the realm of traditional scientific observation.
- In our modern day culture we have been shaped to idolize science-based, evidence-based rational thinking. As a result we have serious issues with this truth layer. But we do need to recognize that this cultural preference for rational evaluation is

a heart-held assumption, a faith-position "i.e. Reason is the only way to truth".

- Here too, it may be necessary to interpret these varied experiences. Are they positive or negative, are they true or false? Is it God or is it Satan, or a self-delusion, or none-of-the-above? For an interpretation, an evaluation, we would need a first principle, an axiom, i.e. a heart-held faith position.

Human experience provides a third layer of truth. To be sure, this layer is much more subjective, much more dependent on personal observations and interpretations (and personal bias). Possibly it would be best to process these experiences, and their truth implications, in community.

Religion is yet again another layer of truth. It is unveiled by spiritually sensitive sages, mystics, many of whom claimed to have heard God or claimed to be speaking for God. (Some humans have a much greater aptitude towards music or art or science, and some are much more attuned to the spiritual realm.) Religion's "basic facts" invariably include first principles and axioms which must be accepted by faith. As argued earlier we cannot step outside of circular reasoning in the field of faith assumptions, in the field of first principles. How, then, do we do reality checks in the area of religion?

To continue with the quote from Bo Bennett, Logically Fallacious

"Some philosophies state that we can never escape circular reasoning because the arguments always come back to axioms or first principles, but in those cases, the circles are very large and do manage to share useful information in determining the truth of the proposition."

Therefore, religion is able to do reality checks by developing a much larger circular reasoning argument, by adding more and more layers of truth: from science, history and experience. The greater the alignment with the other layers the more convincing the truth, the more reasonable the proposition.

Each of the religions, including atheism, would need to add the layers to their circular reasoning argument (seeking to support, to "prove" their faith assumptions, their first principles) and repeatedly ask, "Does this fit seamlessly or is this forced? Is it just spin?" The added layer would, as well, need to be analyzed as to how it tangibly supports the first principle that we are trying to shore up.

Religion's Reality Checks by Adding Layers of Truth

In this section we will mainly focus on the Judeo-Christian story and to a lesser degree the secular atheism story and their foundational faith assumptions. Every adherent of every other religion would need to do the same for their own "truth assumptions" that form the framework for their own cosmic story.

If we simply use the contents of the Bible to prove what the Bible is saying we have a rather small circular reasoning argument. This is done all the time through cross referencing one verse with another verse. It works well in the day to day and in Sunday's sermonizing.

In the same way, if we simply use science's first principle, "Truth is discovered in reason, i.e. science working through the scientific method," to establish what atheists are proclaiming as truth today, we too have a very small circle. (See Petra's and Paula's argument in an earlier section.)

But now and then everyone needs to expand the circle and add other layers of truth: scientific, historical, and empirical (experience) layers. This will never absolutely prove the assumptions for any religion, but it can help us gain more certainty that we are moving in the right direction. If these other layers can only be made to fit into the expanded circle with great difficulty, with questionable intellectual honesty, then we should give pause to reconsider.

Humans have proven themselves excellent at creating the spin that is needed to prove their own personally adopted perspectives (the view they love). We put our intelligence to the test when we attempt to establish proof for the focus on which our heart is set. Who or what we love determines how our mind will argue. The resulting "spin" is a constant trap for us humans. Sometimes, it does seem, we really are too smart for our own good (and too proud to admit it).

ADDING THE LAYER OF SCIENCE TRUTH-FACTS TO "THERE IS A GOD"

Assuming there is a Creator God, can the truth-facts established by science be interpreted to support that assumption? Many scientists give a resounding yes to such an interpretation. (Stone # 8, in a later section, "Twelve Stones" lists several.) They point to the beauty in creation, to the fine-tuning of so many physical laws that make life possible. They look at the encyclopedic information stored in each DNA molecule and ask, "Where did all this information come from?" They look at the seemingly universal moral imprint on the human heart. Believers in God have no problem seeing God's fingerprints everywhere within creation. Is this just spin, or does it fit naturally?

These same truth-facts need to be interpreted by atheists as well using just physics, just evolution, just chance. They, too, need to ask, "Is this just spin, or does it fit naturally?"

ADDING THE LAYER OF HISTORICAL TRUTHS TO "THERE IS A GOD"

Assuming that there is a God who has revealed himself in the Bible, can the historical facts related to the Bible's beginnings and its long journey through the centuries be used to expand and strengthen the circular reasoning argument that God may very well have spoken to us through the Bible? If we add these established historical facts to Peter and Paul's rather weak circular argument (previously presented), we develop a much stronger argument.

Paul: "God must exist."

Peter: "How do you know?"

Paul: "I know because the Bible says so!"

Peter: "How do you know the Bible is true?"

Paul: "The Bible claims to have been written by God through his many prophets. I believe that the history of this amazing book does support that claim."

Peter: "How?"

Paul: "The Bible was written over 1500 years, by over 40 authors from all walks of life, from three different languages, and yet it develops a consistent storyline, the same theme through out. More than that, the Bible has been exposed to the most vicious criticism throughout its long history. Often it has been declared as dead, just a relic from ancient history, yet it has always bounced back. More than that, today people from literally all cultures and languages find in it hope, joy, wisdom and inspiration. We could go on and compare its preservation in terms of accuracy with other ancient texts, even with more recent ones like Shakespeare. There is simply no comparison, the accuracy of the Bible is second to none in spite of its very violent journey through the centuries. We could go on to talk about its influence on the arts, literature, music, architecture, even on the birth of science. Its influence is without comparison. No other book comes even close."

Peter: "I also have heard that the Bible has many prophetic predictions, many of which have already come true. What an amazing history!"

Paul: "Yes, many fulfilled prophecies indeed! I believe it is reasonable to assume that God may very well have had a hand in writing the Bible! Such a one-of-a-kind history would be expected if it were a book with an origin in heaven itself. It is reasonable to assume there is a God because the Bible declares it so."

This is still a circular argument but it has been undergirded significantly by adding a new layer of truth. (A later section, Stone #3, supplements this short discussion.) First principles, assumptions cannot be proved but they can be supported by adding different layers of truth.

There are several other arguments from history that can be added to faith's circular reasoning argument. (Stones # 1- 8 in Part 5 describes these.)

To be sure, atheists have done the same with Petra and Paula's argument mentioned earlier. But in the last analysis it still remains a circular argument and ultimately must be accepted by faith.

It would take a lot of humility, a lot of integrity on all sides to examine where the added information fits seamlessly into the circular argument or where it has been forced. That may never happen (pride is humanity's biggest issue) and so the debate may never begin, most certainly will never end, within culture.

But that does not mean that it cannot end for individual travellers, for small groups of sincere truth seekers on this journey to greater truth, greater confidence!

In addition to the layers of science and history we can also add the layer of empirical (experience) truth.

ADDING THE LAYER OF EMPIRICAL TRUTHS

Assuming there is a God, can human experiences be explained using that assumption? This assumption needs to be accompanied by the assumption that there is a spiritual dimension and that human beings have a soul that can be enlightened to develop an interface with God. Does collective as well as individual experience point to the reasonableness of such an interpretation? We are not attempting to prove this; we are simply attempting to see if reality can be interpreted that way without becoming intellectually dishonest, without creating a spin to make it fit. If that can be done, then that interpretation can be woven into our enlarged circular reason argument for the principle, "There is a God". As a result, our circular reasoning argument would become weightier still.

Let's briefly look at religious experiences generally.

No power has been able to stamp out the religious yearnings of a people. Many have tried. Atheistic Communism's seemingly short run in history attempted to do that, for example in Russia and China. Religious yearnings and all the rituals that go with it are coming back with a surge in these countries.

In western cultures we can see many similar tendencies. Spirituality, once a topic of distain, has become a topic of choice for many retreats and workshops. Churches as well are growing in many places. To be sure they are often filled with older people, and when people are in crisis. This may simply indicate that atheism works well when all is well, but it may not be able to be sustained for the long run. For many young people, cults have become traps, and now we are reading that many are turning to Islam's radical views or to Buddhism's enlightenment ideology to fill some personal need. These contemporary realities may simply be the tip of the iceberg. How many of our young people, older people as well, are struggling with emptiness, with meaninglessness? The lack of spiritual depth in these cases can point to the fact

Obviously not all religious experiences are helpful, many are down right dangerous. To discern how to evaluate religious experiences is beyond the scope of this book. It is a very important topic to be sure (a bit more further down).

that religious experiences may indeed fill a real void within the human heart.

We need to limit our discussion simply to Christianity to consider individual spiritual experiences. Individually, many people report a dynamic relationship with the resurrected Jesus. Many claim to have found forgiveness, peace, joy, meaning and a living hope from this relationship. Many claim to have experienced real life transformation through this relationship with Jesus. This can be seen in all age brackets, from children to seniors. It can be seen in church literature throughout all the centuries. It can be seen in all cultures, across the globe.

The biblical book of Psalms, written 3000 years ago, is a record of the personal and community faith journey. From praise and worship to struggling with life's imponderables, from deep intimacy with God to times of deep distress when God seems altogether distant, from hearts filled with thanksgiving to laments where God simply does not make sense, the full spectrum of Judeo-Christian spiritual experiences are highlighted. Believers through the ages have deeply identified with this collection of heart prayers and songs. This book's broad trans-cultural reception through the millennia, and continuing on today, is proof that the spirituality portrayed in it has validity.

Several books have been included in the reading list to practically illustrate this. The book *Devotional Classics* is a collection of writings from a cross section of people from the many centuries of church history. The reading of these personal writings resonates with Christians today. Our inner experiences, even though we are centuries (as well as cultures) removed, seem so similar. The book *The Question of God* is a wonderful analysis and comparison of two highly intelligent and academic people and their spiritual experiences. C.S. Lewis, an atheist turned believer, and Sigmund Freud, a diehard atheist are illustrated in this very readable book. Their writings and their personal letters describing their joys and struggles in life are simply placed side by side. It is a thought provoking book that affirms the reality of a living, dynamic, faith experience and how this impacts a life. And, by comparison, it illustrates the profound lack created by embracing the atheistic faith.

It is obviously the case that Christian religious experiences exist. Empirical experiences can be added to our circle, in addition to scientific and historical truth, to strengthen the argument even further.

DANGEROUS SPIRITUAL EXPERIENCES

With respect to religious experiences, we need to be aware that our language is full of allusions to a negative reality as well. Witchcraft, demon possession, the occult, trances, hallucinations, séances and many more all suggest that there is a troublesome reality out there beyond the physical that does impact our lives as well. The field of religious experiences, both constructive as well as dangerous, is one to explore with an attitude of humility and integrity, with caution and possibly best with a mature spiritual mentor. Our search for truth in this area of religious experiences is to find that which gives life richness and depth. The search is also necessary to avoid the pitfalls that seem to be present. (To do nothing may not really be an option either; neutrality with respect to this topic may very well be an illusion.)

****

The field of psychology has examined this phenomenon of religious experiences. As a rule, they begin with the assumption that there is no god and no spiritual domain. They typically end with the perspective that these experiences are the result of factors such as cultural brainwashing, parenting, manipulative preachers, misfiring neurons, chemical imbalances within the brain, etc. There may very well be such cases, but to dismiss all religious experiences in this way may be adding a questionable argument (the spin!) to their circular reasoning, in the attempt to shore up their assumptions, their first principles, that there is no god and no spiritual dimension.

Religion's Reality Checks through Careful Responses to Critics

The great problem facing all who are seeking to examine the foundation for their own assumptions is that they cannot escape their own perspective, their own bias. There is a deep desire to have our assumptions indeed be true. We want God to be real. We want the Bible to be true! We can never be completely neutral; we can never be completely open so as to examine the assumptions without a prior commitment to those same premises. (The same is true for the atheists and their assumptions as well.)

Accepting this, we need to be greatly encouraged by our many critics! They do not have our built in biases. As a result they are able to shed a different perspective on our assumptions. By listening carefully to their criticisms, and re-examining our own positions and arguments from their perspectives, we do a more thorough reality check on our own faith foundations. However, it is important to realize that these criticisms may be based on the critic's own biases and assumptions. In fact, one of their biases might very well be, "We don't want God or the Bible to be true".

Christianity has been blessed with many, many critics throughout its long history. As a result Christianity has been able to develop excellent answers to defend its own position. In many cases biblical scholars have as well needed to make adjustments to their biblical interpretations. Over time Christianity's position has become much stronger in the process. The field of apologetics has collected these criticisms as well as all the carefully examined responses to them. Every traveller on the road to a more secure faith needs to have read some of these apologetics books (see reading list).

We need to compare this rich history of criticism within Christianity with that of Islam. In Islam, any criticism, any critic has been silenced through out its long history. Essentially no critic has ever lived long enough to repeat his criticism. The western world, with its value of free speech, is dumbfounded as to how to respond to the adherents of this religion who refuse to look critically at their own faith foundations.

But then the first thing our atheistic culture would need to do is look in the mirror.

Pascal's Wager

We have argued that we can strengthen our assumptions by carefully and honestly adding other layers of truths to create a much greater, much weightier circular argument. We can examine the critics' concerns; these are the only mind-paths we have. We can never rationally prove that God exists, or that any of the other first principles are true, by using any or all of the layers of knowledge accessible to us as humans. Our world is simply larger than our minds can comprehend. There is mystery to our human story. That is a fact. Humanity's searching since the dawn of time is proof of that fact. *We do need to make the leap of faith, but so does everyone else!*

Everyone, including the atheist, must begin with a set of assumptions before they can even begin the reasoning process. Too many people are unaware of these foundational faith assumptions. It is the nature of religion, whether it is atheism or Christianity or Buddhism to elevate these faith assumptions to the status of unquestioned truth.

Our adopted faith propositions must never be equated with facts on par with provable historical and scientific facts. Having admitted to that, it is nevertheless true that faith propositions hold a more foundational stature within our hearts and minds than do verifiable facts. Facts will invariably be interpreted (or twisted) to fit our faith propositions rather than the reverse. The mind, as a rule, serves the heart.

What is needed to break the heart's mold so as to be able to move to a new set of faith propositions? For reflection Matthew 13:10 - 17.

Pascal's Wager has often been presented to the honest (not argumentative) skeptic to give God, to give faith, a chance. There is indeed the possibility that you can find faith simply in the honest living of it. God does meet us where we are. Jesus continues to meet the doubting Thomases. He is able to move us forward from the lowest places possible!

Thomas, one of Jesus' 12 disciples, refused to believe that Jesus had been raised from the dead. The others had all seen him; Thomas had been absent at those times. He refused to believe unless... he himself received multiple concrete proofs himself. Jesus did meet him in his faith struggle (John 20:24).

Blaise Pascal was a devout Christian as well as a genius mathematician during the 17th century. He lived in a time of great skepticism. Medieval orthodoxy and the arguments for the existence for God had been debunked by reason. Reason was beginning to reshape the world after its own image. Faith was at a very low ebb. Pascal used the mathematical theories of probability to develop an argument for faith to help his fellow Parisians come to a similar lively faith as his.

He suggested that each of us has only two options for the biblical claim, "There is a God who promises us forgiveness of sins and life eternal". Which is the better bet, to say "yes" or to say "no"?

We can say, "Yes, there is such a God", resisting all of our doubts in the process. If that is indeed proven to be true, we have gained a very great prize indeed. If it is not true, then we may have lost only a very little, possibly some question-able worldly pleasures for a few years.

We can say that we don't know (agnostic), but this posi-tion is not really possible because not choosing will inevi-tably become a choice that is made for us. If we die as an agnostic, then, in terms of God and Judgment Day, we will have died as an atheist.

We can say, "No, there is no such God". If it turns out that we are indeed right, then we have lost nothing. We may have gained minimally for our very temporary life by not needing to live religiously. If, however, it turns out that we were wrong; and there really is such a God, then we have literally lost everything (and to boot, end up in hell for eternity).

Putting it this way makes atheism really a very poor bet; essentially there is nothing to gain, but possibly everything to lose. And choosing to believe becomes a very, very good bet. We stand to gain everything, but stand to lose, essentially, nothing.

Apply that to a million dollar bet on the toss of a coin, heads you win or tails you lose. You can say, "Forget it I'm not that gullible," or you can say, "Sure, I'll give that a try". How much would you be willing to risk for possibly being found to be gullible? However, how would the too-proud-to-be-gullible guy feel if the other fellow did walk away with a million dollar prize? (Some of the celebrities we worship could easily make such a contest without in the least hurting their financial bottom line!)

Many have dismissed this argument because it caters to our lowest motivations, simply fear and self interest only. Nothing here promotes any degree of love for God or any desire for a more moral life. It is indeed interesting that these critics are concerned about loving God or living a more moral life!

For a fuller treatment of this powerful argument
http://www.peterkreeft.com/ *The Argument from Pascal's Wager*

External / Internal Validation

The Bible claims that the external validation (as best we can) of the Christian faith is followed by an experiential inner validation. The Holy Spirit has been promised to affirm the truth within our own hearts.

"The Spirit testifies with our spirit that we are children of God."
Romans 8:16

This "I know!" reality has been the testimony of the millions who have chosen to follow the Jesus way. An inner certainty is received and stays, that just weeks earlier seemed all but impossible. Many a martyr has gone singing to his/her death buoyed by the overwhelming inner certainty that God is waiting for him/her on the other side.

To begin with, we seek to understand, so that we can find faith. Then we notice that we have moved to a new reality; now, having found faith, we really do understand, more clearly with the mind and even more so with the heart. *It's as though a light has been turned on!* The mind simply responds, "Wow, why couldn't I see this earlier?" And our restless hearts *know* they have found **"home"**!

Confident Faith

Confident faith is evident when faith in God's story is more real than faith in one's own story. Such faith knows that one's personal story, no matter how broken, how uncertain, is embedded in Jesus' Kingdom Story. And his story is as certain as it is historically-rooted, and prophetically-guaranteed.

We should always be careful to critique our own story on the basis of God's Kingdom Story, never the other way around. Using our perplexing experiences as the truth-standard invariably creates a personal faith crisis.

AN HONEST QUESTION

The concern might be raised, "What about adherents of other religions? Many seem to have a similar confidence." This may well be true.

The inner heart confidence that we have, or any adherent of any of the religions has, needs to be exposed to the truth-claims of the other religions. Such a personal or group study needs to be done with an attitude of openness and integrity; honest listening is needed. To want to protect my truth-claims with a critical negative attitude towards the truth-claims under review will only further entrench my biased love for my "truth". An untested inner heart confidence may be a self-delusion. After all, we do live in a world where darkness and light are in a life and death struggle for each of our minds and hearts.

I suspect a person's inner confidence, when tested, will experience a strengthening or an unsettling. The resulting heart condition will suggest the next steps that need to be taken in the search for truth.

Part 3 of this book seeks to provide such an exposure to the many truth-claims battling for supremacy in our troubled world. The secret is to avoid barricading our hearts from the truth-claims of the various religions. Using an analogy from nature, exposing our truth-claims to the elements will either topple the tree or strengthen its roots.

Our western cultures have always considered truth as something abstract, as a philosophical argument, as dogma, or as something that needs to be discovered through hard intellectual work. In the Judeo-Christian worldview, truth is a person (God) who comes looking for us. The unsettling that we experience when exposing ourselves to truth-claims may very well be God speaking to our hearts.

Jesus answered, "I am the Way, The Truth, and the Life." John 14:6

Truth forever on the scaffold, Wrong forever on the throne–
Yet that scaffold sways the future, and, behind the dim unknown,
Standeth God within the shadow, keeping watch above his own.

James Russel Lowell, 1819 – 1891, *The Present Crisis,* Lines 38 – 40.

Men occasionally stumble over the truth, but most of them pick themselves up and hurry off as if nothing ever happened.

Sir Winston Churchill, British World War 2 Prime Minister, *(1874 – 1965).*

PATHWAY TO CONFIDENCE

1. Empowering Spirituality

2. Cultural Awareness

3. Religious Literacy

4. Validating our Faith Assumptions

5. *Encountering the Kingdom Story*

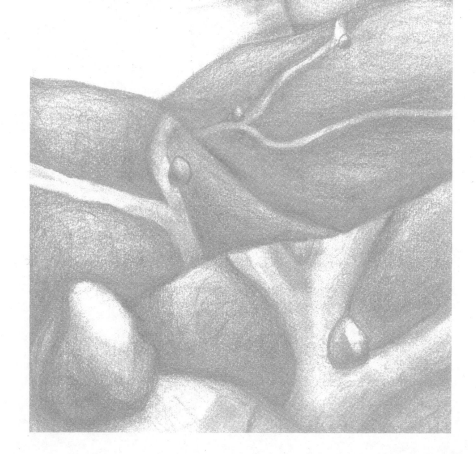

Part 5: Encountering the Kingdom Story

a few thoughts to begin with...

Many of us may have grown up with the Bible stories. Bedtime stories, Sunday School lessons and sermonettes may have shaped us to think of the Bible as a collection of stories from Adam and Eve, to Noah, Joseph, Daniel, Jesus, Peter and Paul and so many more. We may have become so familiar with this multitude of stories that we may never have really been impacted by the one grand story where all of these are really only the characters and punctuation marks that move the story along. We may have lost sight of the forest (or may never even have seen it) by focusing on the individual trees. It is this grandest of all stories that needs to be encountered in a deeper way.

Read the next story, the Judeo-Christian story, in one sitting. Read it several times, over several days, if need be, until the scope and magnitude, the breadth and depth begin to register.

Read this cosmic story with the heart. Listen for the deeper stirrings that may be brought to the surface. In our culture we have trained the mind to interrupt, to critique, to take charge, to change the focus when it should be made to stand aside until the heart has begun to understand. It is only afterwards that the mind is needed to help put words and perspective to what has been heard.

There is a deeper knowing where the mind can only play catch up. There is a deeper listening where the mind is only a bystander. We are in the dimension where an appreciation for beauty is recognized but words are lacking to describe it, where a love that cannot be rationalized matures, where error is sensed and truth is affirmed before it can even begin to be understood.

Psalm 42:7
"Deep calls to deep   (God's heart to my heart)
  in the roar of your waterfalls;
    all your waves and breakers
      have swept over me."

The Psalmist has attempted to use words and metaphor to explain a heart encounter with deity – the One "in whom we live and move and have our being" (Acts 17:28); the One who ever seeks to break through all the barriers that we have built in our attempt to hide our broken selves from him.

The Judeo-Christian Meta-Story

Start to read at bottom left corner

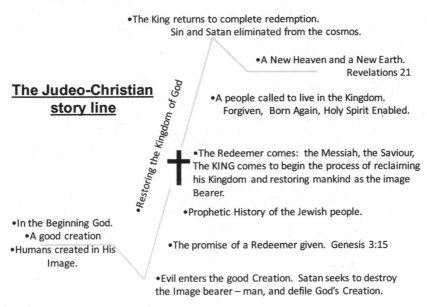

•The King returns to complete redemption.
Sin and Satan eliminated from the cosmos.

•A New Heaven and a New Earth.
Revelations 21

**The Judeo-Christian
story line**

•Restoring the Kingdom of God

•A people called to live in the Kingdom.
Forgiven, Born Again, Holy Spirit Enabled.

•The Redeemer comes: the Messiah, the Saviour,
The KING comes to begin the process of reclaiming
his Kingdom and restoring mankind as the image
Bearer.

•Prophetic History of the Jewish people.

•In the Beginning God.
•A good creation
•Humans created in His
Image.

•The promise of a Redeemer given. Genesis 3:15

•Evil enters the good Creation. Satan seeks to destroy
the Image bearer – man, and defile God's Creation.

PREAMBLE

Genesis chapters 1 - 9 give us a short introduction to the biblical sto-ryline. Christians have long been drawn into heated battles as to the nature of these classic chapters of beginnings. Is it factual history? Is it science? Or is it myth, simply one more among the many creation myths of ancient literature? The argument will never be decided in debate; no one was there to observe. And, the Bible does not really address that question anywhere to our satisfaction. Science may suggest some clues. Archeology gives facts; history suggests others. All of these facts must be interpreted. These interpretations invariably are in keeping with the assumptions and perspectives we begin with.

Genesis 1 – The classic 6 day Creation Story.
Genesis 2 – Creation of humankind – male and female.
Genesis 3 – The temptation in the garden – the fall of man.
Genesis 4 – Cain and Abel – the first murder, cultural brokenness, sin takes root in all aspects of life.
Genesis 5 – Genealogy – Adam to Noah – the family's flaw spreads.
Genesis 6 - 9 – Noah's flood – Judgment and Redemption themes foreshadowed.

Arguments as to how these chapters are to be harmonized with history or science have proven to be a major distraction to the real issues raised by these chapters. Too much time and energy has been spent on these questions. Too many thoughtful people have rejected the whole story on the basis of over-confident claims about the nature of these opening episodes.

Genesis Chapters 1- 9 are first and foremost religious in nature. They provide, in story form, the biblical framework for answering the ultimate life questions. These chapters introduce us to the main characters, the setting, the plot, and the theme of the biblical meta-story. It is into this framework of beginnings that this amazing biblical, historically rooted meta-story unfolds. We do, first and foremost, need to focus on the religious worldview facts that these ancient chapters make with such simple yet elegant brushstrokes. These chapters really are without comparison within the genre of ancient literature.

CREATION, FALL, REDEMPTION, RESTORATION
(a four term overview of the biblical story)

The first verse, "In the beginning God created..." introduces us to God, the hero of this grand story. He is the Creator of all the cosmos. God is Spirit, therefore, the spiritual dimension gives birth to the material physical world and everything in it. God simply speaks it into existence, one element at a time, till the miracle planet floats in space, in all its splendor, surrounded by myriad galaxies.

The issues as to how long a process creation was and the method as to how it was created have caused all the fuss. The key point is simply that God created. That truth must be emphasized. The rest must not be allowed to become a distraction to this main truth.

God made it all! The spiritual supports and sustains the physical and all the life forms that it contains. The cosmos is like a simple cloud that materializes out of the clear blue sky. The invisible sky gives substance to, carries, and supports the cloud and can just as well simply cause it to disappear again.

The physical, that which is visible, is completely dependent on the spiritual, the invisible. This is fundamental to the whole story line. Planet Earth is not merely an open system but also a completely dependent system. The breakdown of this relationship, between the spiritual and the material, between God and man, is the root of all that ails the planet.

This truth is reflected in our day to day. It was Rene Descarte, often considered the Father of Modernism (d. 1650), who said, "I think therefore I am, <u>Cogito ergo sum</u>." Reason has since become paramount in our culture. But, this may prove to be the epic error of modernism. Our success, our happiness, our wellbeing is not as dependent on what we know as it is on **who** we know. Relationship is at the root of our wellbeing. The truth is much closer to, "I love therefore I am." What or who we love shapes our destiny far more than what we know. Our mind and reason are servant to the heart. The mind will dream up hundreds of reasons why we should follow a certain pathway, and twist many facts in the process, if our heart is set on it. Who or what we love; relationship is key!

Smith, *Desiring the Kingdom*, has developed this well.

This world belongs to God. He created it. It is his Kingdom. It reflects his wisdom, his love of beauty, harmony, plenty, and shalom.

God created this awe inspiring place, this garden of bliss, for the visual display of his glory.

Genesis 1 introduces us, next, to the focus character of the story – humanity. The story adopts an ancient near eastern mindset to show a God who created the garden like a temple and finished it by placing his "idol", his representative, into it as its crowning centre piece.

Shalom is the traditional Hebrew greeting meaning "Wishing you God's blessings for complete harmony within all of your surroundings and relationships, perfect peace and plenty at every level of your being."

Life's Ultimate Questions: Exploring the Stories that Shape Our Everyday

Humans were installed as God's image, God's reflection, God's under-kings on planet earth. God's plan was to be "visibly present" through humanity, through you and me.

The "idol", the image, created to visibly represent God in the cosmos, not to be worshipped but to worship the LORD of All.

Humanity's heart focus was to "love God with all of its heart, soul, mind and strength" (Mark 12:30). Our assignment was first and fore-most to represent him, to reflect his moral character within the cosmos. Our task was to tend and complete the garden that God had started. We were to be the caretakers of all that belongs to God. The human family was to be a blessing to all other living things, to animals and plants alike. The few acres of Shalom-Eden were to become a Shalom-Planet, a testa-ment to God's wisdom, love and faithfulness. The chapter ends with the hope that it would be an "and they (Adam and Eve) lived happily ever after" story.

We were created in his image. We humans were created to tell the truth about God in all we are and do. Love of truth, faithfulness in relationship, compassion towards all, creativity in shaping the physical planet, a passion for beauty, order, diversity, harmony etc. The universe and beyond, all living things, both physical and spiritual, angels and demons, are watching! Shakespeare was correct; the world's a stage for the greatest drama ever within time and space.

This creation story answers so many of life's ultimate questions for this worldview, this religion. It begins to answer key questions such as
- What is God like?
- What does it mean to be human?
- What is the meaning of life?
- What is our purpose and our task?
- What gives us humans our dignity?
- What is the true wellspring of our lives, our wellbeing?

This creation story firmly underlines the truth that our earthly home is an awesome and good world and that God is a wise, almighty, and good ruler over all. It affirms that above all, his blessing is most to be desired.

Male and Female

Genesis 2 introduces us to that most unique relationship built into creation, into the human experience. Male and female, together and interdependent, reflect, to a deeper level, what it means to be God's image bearers. God is first of all a God who seeks relationship. God is perfect love and exercises covenant faithfulness. Not only are we, as humans, to reflect this to the whole cosmos, we are also to experience it within our own unique soul-mate and family relationships. From within this male-female relationship we are to reflect more of God's moral perfection. This male-female covenant relationship is God's Michelangelo, God's

Rembrandt, God's masterpiece! Is it any wonder why sincere adherents of this worldview gasp in shock and horror at the ease with which our culture is redefining our sexuality and marriage!

Creation Illustrates Spiritual Truths

The truth that mankind is created in God's image suggests that much of creation is created to illustrate spiritual realities. When we are puzzled by a specific spiritual reality, it is good to ask, "What did God create within the physical dimension to illustrate that truth?" For example, why is the Holy Spirit symbolized as fire? God created fire to help us understand the work and function of the Holy Spirit. Like fire, the Holy Spirit gives light and warmth; the Holy Spirit exposes impurities. In another example, Jesus points us to the classic "redemption through sacrificial death" truth that lies at the heart of the Judeo-Christian meta-story. Every springtime seed must first sacrifice itself and die before it can bring forth new life (John 12:24). Creation illustrates spiritual truths on its every page!

Jesus, the Master Teacher employs this principle in all of his parables. Each parable is an illustration of a spiritual truth embedded in the created order.

CREATION, **FALL**, REDEMPTION, RESTORATION

Chapters 1 and 2 introduced us to the setting and the characters of the story. Genesis 3 continues the story by illustrating, with simple brush-strokes, what has gone so very, very wrong on Planet Earth. The plot, the problem that needs to be overcome, is presented as a simple story that even a child can understand.

Just a few times within the biblical record do we see the curtain drawn back to give us humans a glimpse of the much larger struggle within the cosmos, of which our struggles are but a shadow; the first few chapters of Job, Isaiah 14:11-13, the stories surrounding Jesus in the gospels, the book of Revelation, and here in Genesis chapter 3 are the major passages. We become aware that we humans are, what must seem to so many, just pawns in the cosmic struggle between good and evil, between God and Satan. Many, many questions remain. The Bible's near silence on so many of these questions suggests that the dimensions of this cosmic moral battle are beyond our ability to comprehend. The human response that we are repeatedly challenged to make involves faith and trust in a loving sovereign God rather than understanding. Relationship, not knowledge, is the primary key!

Understanding Satan

Satan, created as a magnificent angelic spiritual creature, has become God's arch-rival for control of planet earth. Satan's main focus is to destroy the image bearer, God's representative, humankind, you and me. His main strategy is to create a wedge of distrust, of disobedience in the all important God-human relationship. Through questioning of God's goodness, through temptation to turn away from God, Satan has succeeded in severing the life-sustaining relationship between Creation and God. The consequences are ever-widening and all-consuming cycles of death and destruction for the human race and, as a result, for creation over which they were to rule under God. The rest of the book of Genesis records this downward spiral into dysfunction, brokenness and death. The bent towards evil has become rooted in the heart of the human family. No one can escape this downward pull towards rebellion to the Creator, towards self-centeredness and self-destruction.

Modern reason has serious issues with this assertion of a personal evil reality, i.e. the devil. We do need to consider; it is through human agency that this evil works, so often behind the scenes, so often cloaked as a simple human being. In extreme situations we say the person is "possessed".

Understanding Evil

How should we understand the evil that seems to crop up everywhere and destroy so much? The Bible is clear, Satan cannot create anything new. Only God can create and he pronounced everything good. Evil is best understood as the corruption of the good that God created. We need only stop to consider how often that which is so good can end up being so destructive: relationships, our sexuality, drugs, alcohol, technologies, leadership etc. If used correctly, all of these can be such a profound blessing in our lives; if misused, so destructive. Understood this way suggests that the presence of God in our lives enables the correct use of these good creation gifts; the so often disguised influence of Satan encourages their misuse.

Now that the relationship between God and humanity has been stressed if not severed, the personal evil force, called Satan, and his spiritual forces, influence if not invade the vacant human heart. Through human agency he creates the havoc that he does. One needs only to consider the historical realities of the horrific evil unleashed by Hitler, or Stalin, or contemporary terrorists, or any of the other "monsters" within our societies and we are forced to ask, how could one person have possibly caused so much evil? The Bible's assertion of a hidden, behind the scenes personal evil power that "haunts" individuals provides a most plausible answer.

Satan, having successfully severed humanity from God, gains moral authority over the cosmos. What had been God's good kingdom, with humans exercising stewardship and dominion, has become Satan's dominion, his kingdom, with humanity in bondage to his authority. Our human struggle to pursue enduring lasting good is an ongoing challenge with temporary success at best. Our struggle to keep chaos at bay is short-lived. Our best efforts inevitably fall short and ultimately fail. Continual struggle and finally death become our universal destiny with the greatest of certainty. We have been cut off from the life-giving resources of the Creator God, expelled from this life-sustaining relationship, and banished into an endless, hopeless struggle for survival that inevitably ends in death.

Humanity, collectively, deeply recognizes that somehow our root problem is our relationship with deity. On this all the classic religions agree. Within our hearts we carry the imprint of our good creation. We long for justice, goodness, peace, love, life but, alas, these remain so frequently out of reach in spite of our very best efforts. Life has become a journey of broken dreams for all.

Understanding what it means to be Human

Humans, the Bible asserts, were created to be enlivened with a spiritual reality, i.e. the presence, the breath of God within. The Hebrew word for Spirit is "breath." The answer that is suggested for, "How much do we need God?" is, "As much as we need that next breath!" Even the exclusive personal name of God, YHWH, (Yahweh) simply uses soft consonants that create a breath-like word. There are no sharp, hard consonants. This is another beautiful example where creation (in this case language) illustrates spiritual truth.

Understanding Suffering

Mankind's most desperate question is that of suffering. How can an all-powerful as well as an all-loving deity allow suffering? Why did he even create a world where suffering is possible? The answer, to a degree at least, is found in the dynamics of a loving relationship. God created us for such a relationship. True love needs free choice and the context within which to exercise that choice. Without the ability to say 'no' to God, we would simply have been emotional robots. God, in his wisdom, knew that the joys of eternal intimacy with him would far outweigh the sorrows of an, in comparison, short lifetime. This, God asks us to accept by faith.

Science and medicine can measure and control the pain. Suffering is often simply the mental and heart anguish associated with all of these questions. Just to find an answer can resolve so much of this suffering.

A culture that endorses fun and pleasure as its ultimate good, does find suffering a decidedly bitter pill to swallow. But it is suffering itself that may be able to convince some that culture's values are out of line with reality. Suffering may be needed to help discover the more important dimensions of life. (All religions agree, suffering can 'force' deeper insights.)

When we, as friends and family, patiently walk with those who suffer then our higher human values are encouraged to rise to the top. Compassion, empathy, love and faithfulness can be on full display when we respond humanely to neighbours in need. Such responses invariably create headlines in our shallow culture.

The Bible's answer to suffering ultimately centres on the person of Jesus Christ. He came into our pain to suffer with, and ultimately for, us. His actions speak greater comfort than any words could possibly say.

Those who sit on the sidelines of suffering invariably struggle with the question, "Why would a loving God...?" Believers who are in the throws of suffering, struggle, too, but often find a growing peace in the closeness of relationship with deity. Many non-believers as well have found their way back to God through the gateway of suffering. Instead of giving in to bitterness, a heart response of acceptance and trust in the sovereignty and love of God has birthed comfort and peace, if not joy and hope, within many a broken heart and body. Relationship and trust, not reason and knowledge, paradoxically lead to growing victory in the face of these difficult obstacles.

CREATION, FALL, **REDEMPTION**, RESTORATION

The Genesis story continues to lay the groundwork for the greatest of all stories ever told. Into this saddest of all stories, God speaks hope. Genesis 3:15 begins the long journey towards redemption of all that had been lost. A redeemer is promised, someone who will destroy Satan and restore mankind's fortunes.

God speaking to Satan
"And I will put enmity
between you and the woman,
and between your offspring and hers;

> he will crush your head,
> and you will strike his heel." Genesis 3:15

This redemption theme becomes the focus for all of the remaining chapters of the Bible till all is accomplished. The enemy's head is crushed. The enemy is destroyed. Mankind is redeemed and God is glorified, now not only in creation but now, all the more in redemption as well! This may very well be the overarching reason why the story, with all of its pain and suffering, was deemed necessary by an almighty, sovereign, all-wise deity. (For reflection: Revelation chapters 4 and 5, worship inspired by creation and redemption.)

Over the many chapters of biblical history, more information is repeatedly presented as to the nature of this redeemer and the redemption that will be accomplished. Some have counted over 300 prophecies with many more allusions that point to the One that was to come. The history of the Jewish people becomes the setting into which all of these prophesies are presented and recorded. At the very core of the children of Abraham lies the hope that someday someone will come to restore all that was lost. The very culture of the Jewish people has been shaped by the giving and unfolding of these prophecies. The seven annual biblical feasts, embedded in the Jewish calendar, tell the story of redemption history, from start to finish. (See Stone # 5 in the following section.)

The four gospels, the good news of Jesus, give us the biography of the One who was so long awaited. His life story...
- begins with a few glimpses into his mysterious conception and birth,
- to a few brief episodes of his childhood,
- to a more detailed overview of his actions and his teachings during his short three-year public ministry.
- A full one third of this amazing gospel record details a day by day coverage of his last week,
- and then culminates in a word for word, moment by moment, account of his death.

Life's Ultimate Questions: Exploring the Stories that Shape Our Everyday

Attention is above all, focused on his death! How unique, how different this is from any biography of any other man who has shaped the chapters of human history! The gospel story closes with the unbelievable declaration that he did indeed rise from the dead and that his death and resurrection have somehow become the all-sufficient key for redemption of the human family and all creation alike.

The gospels tell the story; they make this seemingly unbelievable claim. The rest of the New Testament interprets the story and places it into the context of the greater meta-story, the worldview, the religion that has now circumvented the globe so often simply by word of mouth sharing, so often by skeptics turned believers, so often by men and women who paid the martyrs price in the telling.

The dilemma in which human kind finds itself, according to this meta-story, is galaxies removed from anything that the human family could solve on its own. Herein lies the uniqueness and the controversy surrounding this story.

- No amount of suffering, not even many lifetimes of suffering, could resolve the justice issues raised in the God-man relational breakdown. (Hinduism — karma)
- No amount of enlightenment (Buddhism) or education (Modernism) can transform the moral character issues needed for a return to relationship with deity.
- No amount of obedience to religious protocols and moral self-effort on humanity's part can undo the bent towards evil that is inborn in the heart of every man, women, and child. (Islam)
- And according to the biblical meta-story, no amount of evolutionary progress, even with humanity's participation as technological agents, will be sufficient to make a way towards the taming of the wilderness within our aching hearts and on this "angry planet". The growing pessimism in culture, as our planet and the human family hurtle towards catastrophic failures on so many fronts, is confirming this sentiment already.

The problem facing the human family is beyond anything that can be solved without divine help. A redeemer needed to be sent from heaven itself!

Jesus' resurrection is presented as proof not only that he was the one that was promised so very long ago, but that he was also God who took on human form; divine help for a problem only deity could solve.

It could be argued, and often is, that the Jesus story just reflects the ancient myths. In these myths the gods and goddesses were continually and critically involved in all of the affairs of men. But the reverse could just as easily be argued. All of these ancient myths simply reflect the sentiment of all men. Divine help is needed if mankind's situation is ever to be improved. Any person who has reflected deeply on the ageless/endless human dilemma and tragedy would be challenged to provide another "no-god" solution. Jesus has become that all-sufficient divine help that humanity has longed for, as reflected in so much of ancient literature.

* **His teachings** provide instruction and correction for humankind's universal and never-ending search for deity and for guidance to help us live in relationship with our Creator God.

** **He modeled** for us how humankind was created to live. He displayed a total dependence on, and complete obedience to, the spiritual dimension, his Father in Heaven. Even though in essence he was divine, he lived on earth as fully human, as one of us, albeit fully supported by the spiritual dimension. He modeled the life we were created to live.

*** **His human life**, lived perfectly, is credited to us, because perfection alone permits reinstatement into relationship with God.

> God made him who had no sin to be sin for us so that in him we might become the righteousness of God. 2 Corinthians 5:21 (Often called the Great Exchange)

To enable this perfect human life and fully human death as our representative, Jesus needed to share completely in our humanity, hence the mysterious teachings surrounding the virgin birth and the dual nature (divine and human), within the person of Jesus.

**** **His human death**, unjustly served, is credited to us because a Holy God of a moral universe must execute sentence for rebellion against the divine order. God takes upon himself, through Jesus Christ, the burden of our sin. Divine love was willing to satisfy the demands of a just and holy moral universe. This path is beyond anything we humans could ever understand. The Bible simply proclaims from cover to cover that "there is no forgiveness of sins without the shedding of blood," (the giving or taking of life) Hebrews 9:22.

***** **His death as a perfect man**, as our representative, breaks the curse, humanity's and creation's bondage to Satan's authority.

This talk about blood being essential for salvation is difficult for modern man to accept. Possibly we have just become too civilized. The following truth may help. The protein on our dinner plate comes to us seasoned and shrink-wrapped in plastic. We seldom consider that this meat represents an animal that had to die; its blood had to be shed so that we could be nourished physically. It is easier to go from a deep awareness that an animal needed to die so that I might live physically, to believing that Jesus' death is key to life spiritually.

****** **In his resurrection**, he becomes for us, the first renewed man. Humankind needed more than a new beginning, a clean slate, another try. Humanity needed the imparting of spirit-life. The spirit connection with God, the key to all that is wrong, is restored within the core of our being. Essentially in Jesus the human family is "reborn" (with spiritual DNA restored) and all who say yes to Jesus enter into this new family (Romans 5:12-19).

This spiritual reality — what we are becomes credited to him, and what he is and has done becomes ours — does have its shadows in our world. Seldom does one succeed or fall by himself. Many share in the consequences, either good or bad. This is particularly true in the context of family and this often for generations to come. Many other areas of life could be used to illustrate this phenomenon as well; we are in most situations together whether we want to or not. (Is individualism, to a large degree, an illusion?)

We do need to carefully choose who we follow, the team to which we belong, the relationships we develop. The choice will, so often, determine whether we sink or swim.

Jesus names this radical transformation a being born again. The prophet Jeremiah described it as a heart transplant. The apostle Paul likens it to dying and being reborn, a being adopted into a new family. It is a spiritual being-born-again. We are legally reckoned to have died with him and then raised with him. We have become spiritually renewed in him. The spiritual dimension can again support the physical. This new beginning results in new sensitivities, appetites and potentials.

Jesus' teachings, his life, and his death and resurrection have become for us the pathway to wholeness, the pathway to restoration of all that had been lost. We enter this pathway through faith, simply accepting what God has provided. A gift so undeserved, so divine, can be ours simply by faith, and by faith alone. Any attempt on our part to think that we can or need to earn it or that we somehow deserve it, is to declare that we have not yet understood the depths of our problem, nor the magnitude of his gift.

> What makes the Christian story so unique? The gift of salvation is by grace alone, undeserved and unearned; it is received simply by turning our broken selves expectantly towards him. God's hand of compassionate love is extended to us no matter how far we have fallen. He picks us up no matter how deep the hole is that we have dug for ourselves. Grace meets us where we are! But grace does not leave us there. It ever seeks to move us towards the true destiny for which we were originally created, where freedom is defined not as a license to do as I want, but as the power to do as I ought.

CREATION, FALL, REDEMPTION, **RESTORATION**

We are nearing the end of the story. The Bible calls it the new age or the age to come. It has already dawned in the resurrection of Jesus and in every heart that has begun the transforming relationship with Jesus. The problem began in the heart of the human family, in Adam and Eve. Restoration begins in the hearts of people who by faith and trust in

Jesus have begun the journey to wholeness, through the indwelling Holy Spirit. The spiritual dimension is again beginning to nurture and sustain the physical. The fruit of the Spirit – love, joy, peace, patience, goodness, kindness, faithfulness, gentleness, and self-control are beginning to again be reflected in the lives of those who are learning to walk as Jesus walked (Galatians 5:22). The image of God is beginning to show again. God's goal from the beginning has always been to be "visibly present" on planet earth through his image bearer — mankind. Redeemed humanity is again being called to be agents of change and healing on Planet Earth. The future final restoration is casting shadows backwards in time through the renewal at work within many a human heart.

A very important question in any worldview discussion is to ask, "Where are we on the story line graph of the particular religion under discussion?" Christianity is often held hostage to the obvious fact that the world is still a very, very troubled place. Nothing seems to have been changed! Jesus seems to have been an utter failure! We need to remember, though, that the Christian story line is not yet at the place where Jesus will return and personally reign on planet earth. At that point in the story all the evil will have been removed. Till then, the focus of Jesus' work is simply the human heart (the root of the problem). True followers of Jesus are challenged to impact others and culture within their sphere of influence.

The seed (truths that set men free) has been sown and germination happens in the struggle deep within the darkness of our own broken hearts. The influence of God's Spirit in our hearts, at the core of our being, needs to begin to impact all of our relationships – our work and play, our interactions with the environment, our care of animals and plants and resources alike. What became ours legally when by faith we said yes to Jesus, needs to become ours behaviorally. Our lives will reflect, to an ever increasing extent, the spiritual reality of our union with Christ.

We continue to walk by faith in Jesus when discouraged by the slowness of change within. There is much within our own hearts that clouds our eyes with tears. Much within our actions will need radical transformation. This is no instant overnight transformation but the process of a lifetime. Key here is to understand that God the Spirit is not the one who changes us unilaterally but the one who ever seeks to make us partners with him for all the changes that are needed. We continue to be so slow, often so reluctant, in our willingness to be partners with him. Over time, though, we can look back over our lives and we begin to see the changes in character that he has enabled. Hope continues because God has promised to finish what he has started. Restoration will continue in an ever increasing number of hearts of men and women, to an ever greater degree in these hearts, and when we pass through the curtain of death, or when Jesus returns, transformation will be completed in the twinkling of an eye.

The New Testament book of Romans is the most organized theological book in the New Testament yet it does not directly mention heaven (in the sense of us going to heaven). In so much of Christendom today the gospel has been reduced to simply going to heaven. In Romans, as in the rest of the New Testament, the primary focus is all about being one with Christ, living as he would live, being energized by his Spirit, living as we were created to live, as true image bearers (reflections) of the Holy Creator. "Heaven" is but the assumed end-goal!

The promise of Jesus' return, no more to suffer and die for sins but to fully reclaim and restore the Kingdom that had been lost, is the hope that sustains his people during the dying days of Satan's reign on Planet

Earth. The spiritual victory that was won with blood so many centuries ago will come with power and with speed when Jesus returns.

A NEW HEAVEN AND A NEW EARTH

The biblical meta-story promises a new heaven and a new earth. The old, so marred by sin, will be renewed, recreated to the core. Paradise lost will be paradise regained! All that was lost in Genesis will be restored. Humanity's longing for true and lasting intimacy will be perfectly realized in the God-human spiritual bond. Intimacy, with complete acceptance, deepest belonging, and unconditional, covenant love is our greatest need.

Inherent in this God-human bond is the fulfillment of the "Mother of all Promises".

Many have found, even on this side of eternity, great comfort, deep meaning and a lasting cure for the loneliness epidemic of our existence in this relationship with Jesus. Marriage was created to be but a simple reflection of what true intimacy is.

> "I will live with them and walk among them,
> and I will be their God, and they will be my people."
> 2 Corinthians. 6:16

The dignity of mankind will be fully restored; no longer will we seem to be the curse on creation. We will become the blessing-giver for all God's creatures. We will reflect God's holy moral character perfectly in all of our interactions with everyone and everything on recreated Planet Earth.

Our dreams, our deepest longings for life after death, lasting shalom, significance and meaning will be perfectly satisfied, never to be lost again. Redeemed humanity will be confirmed in righteousness. The path to wholeness after all, during this age of decision, is through discipleship, through transformation initiated by personal choice. When Jesus returns God will confirm the choices we have made in our pathway through life (whether they are for or against).

The last chapter of the Bible echoes the losses of the opening chapters of Genesis.

> And I heard a loud voice from the throne saying, "Look! God's dwelling place is now among the people and he will dwell with them. They will be his people, and God himself will be with them and be their God. He will wipe every tear from their eyes. There will be no more death or mourning or crying or pain, for the old order of things has passed away." He who was seated on the throne said, "I am making everything new!" Then he said, "Write this down, for these words are trustworthy and true." Revelation 21:3-5

It was C.S. Lewis who said that there are two kinds of people; those who say to God, "Your will be done" and those to whom God says, "Your will be done." God created humanity with the freedom of choice. He will respect our choices on Judgment Day.

These verses make it very clear that our eternal future is not one of sitting on the clouds playing harps in God's presence (as Hollywood depicts it and as so much popular Christianity seems to teach). We will not live where God lives; he will live with us where we live, on recreated Planet Earth. (But what will this "physical" planet be like when the spiritual dimension will again be foundational as well as "visibly" present?)

This blessed future we all long for is buried deep within the hearts of every man, woman, and child who has ever walked this planet. No burden of tragedy and suffering, of struggle and failure has been able to erase this longing. Deep within each one of us lies the creation promise. *We were meant for so much more than has become of us, on this painful*

...

journey through life. Death and the ever downward spiral of all that we are and attempt and have, as universal as it is, nevertheless seems like such a cursed contradiction to the dreams (really memories of something lost) that we all carry so very deep in our souls.

The biblical meta-story says **Yes and Amen** not to the universality of death and loss, but to those dreams, those memories of better things that we all carry so deep within. We continue hoping against all hope, even to our last dying breath, that they may yet come true. Jesus is the key to the eternal fulfillment of those deepest of dreams and longings.

The Bible story closes with one last passion-filled prayer, a yearning for the conclusion of all that has been promised.

> The Spirit and the bride say, "Come!" And let the one who hears say, "Come! Let the one who is thirsty come; and let the one who wishes take the free gift of the water of life," Revelation 22:17. "Amen, come Lord Jesus." Revelation 22:20

The Spirit, in this last prayer is the yearning of God, the true hero of the story, who longs for this story to find its promised fulfillment. The bride who has come to share this longing with God is none other than redeemed humanity. After all, this meta-story is the greatest love story of all time beyond any that could ever have been imagined! God the Creator and Father of us all is seeking to restore his true love to himself. And what a price he was willing to pay, what a path he was willing to walk, to make it come true for you and for me!

BEFORE WE LEAVE THIS STORY!

This meta-story from Genesis to Revelation has such a simple story line that even a child can understand. Yet it is one that has inspired the greatest and most enduring literature, art, music, architecture, etc. of all time. Myriads of people, from all walks of life and all cultures and historical time periods, credit their transformation of character, and hope-filled, confident expectations, no matter how dark their present may be, on this story. The One who made it all possible, Jesus, continues to speak words of invitation to one and all.

"Come to me, all you who are weary and burdened, and I will give you rest." Matthew 11:28

AN INVITATION TO CONSIDER

We live in a culture that celebrates choice. We can choose this or that, we can choose to agree or disagree. We can choose yes or no. And our culture adds, "To each his own, perfect freedom for all."

As a result we consider the invitation of Jesus as simply another one of those choices that we can take or leave, thank you very much.

But there are choices that have consequences for time and eternity! The King's gentle invitation may very well be our command! Indeed, in a sense, it will be the only criteria on Judgment Day. Either we will stand alone to give account, or we will stand with Jesus who will simply respond, "This one is one of mine!"

LIFE'S ULTIMATE QUESTIONS
FROM JUDEO-CHRISTIANITY'S PERSPECTIVE

- The Question of Truth — The Foundational Question.
  - Truth is revealed in the Bible, illustrated in Creation.
  - Truth is revealed in history. Jesus is God in human form (incarnation). He reveals to us God's heart, his love for us.

> Many people stumble over the problem, "How could God have lived as a human being on planet earth?" These people miss the point. The much bigger problem is, "Why would God go to such an extreme to rescue us rebels who, adding insult to injury, continue to spurn him?"

- The Questions Surrounding our Humanity.
  - Humanity's dignity is rooted in the "created in God's image" truth. A human life, from its beginning to its end, is sacred (to murder is an affront to God himself).
  - Life is all about re-establishing relationship with God.
  - Life is all about becoming like Jesus in our moral character.
  - Our participation in furthering the Kingdom of God is to shape all of our activities, from family and career, to civic involvements and creation care.

- The Question of Ethics.
  - Love, Marriage (male and female) and Family are to be valued and are to be an illustration to us, as well as others, of God's love, faithfulness, and goodness.
  - There is a moral imprint within our hearts, i.e. our conscience, as a guide for ethics. This is to be corrected by God's revealed Word.

- The Questions Surrounding Evil and Suffering.
  - The relational breakdown between God and man has given Satan entrance into the human story. Satan works, so often behind the scenes, through the agency of humans, to create more and more chaos.
  - Suffering is inevitable because the spiritual dimension (God) no longer is in sync with the physical dimension (caused by human rebellion against the divine order: sin).
  - Suffering creates a huge moral problem because the Bible teaches both, a God who is all-powerful as well as all-good. We need to keep these two truths about God in tension. Together they reveal that there is much that we as humans simply cannot understand about God and this moral universe.

216

- The Questions Surrounding the Future.
  - Everyone lives once. Judgment Day follows the end of time.
  - Judgment will ultimately be based on our acceptance or denial of Jesus. Either we have allowed him to take the consequences of our sinfulness or we will bear it alone on the day on which we will need to give account.
  - Eternal life with God and everything good, or hell (life separated from God and everything good), awaits us all.

Twelve Stones – a Basic Apologetic for the Judeo-Christian Faith

There are several wonderful stories in the Old Testament about the keeping-the-faith journey. The children of Israel experienced a great visitation from God, possibly a miraculous rescue or a power encounter. At such times God often told the Israelites to build a memorial, in one case a monument of 12 stones, one for each of the twelve tribes (Joshua 4:19-24). These stones were to be a concrete reminder of this great faith-enriching encounter with God. Whenever God seemed distant, or when the faith to keep going was weak or stressed, then this monument would serve as a reminder to stay the course, to keep plodding along life's faith journey, even in the face of seemingly contradictory stumbling blocks.

Our faith journey is indeed a journey that requires faith from start to finish. There will be times when our faith is challenged severely, there will be times when God seems distant, if not non-existent, and there will be times when we do experience the "dark night of the soul" as the Christian mystics used to call it. There will even be times when God simply does not make sense rationally. Such a Job-experience is a well documented experience for many believers through the ages. These struggles are a given for every true follower of Jesus.

Job is one of the books of the Bible. It tells the story of Job, a righteous man, who experienced the greatest of struggles with God. His faith was challenged to the breaking point. He suffered the loss of all his family, his wealth, and finally his health. For 36 chapters righteous Job rails against his "friends" who charge him with hiding secret sins for such "obvious punishment" from God, and finally Job rails against God who seems to have forgotten him completely when he needed him most.

When God does respond to Job, he simply insists that Job must trust even when he does not understand. God makes no attempt to help Job understand. He is simply encouraged to trust. God's answer in short is, "You, a mere mortal, cannot even understand the physical world. How could you possibly think that you can understand the moral universe?" And having encountered God, Job does learn to trust without understanding. Every Christian, too, must learn that lesson. So many of our paths will seem like dark, dark valleys till we do. God's ways with us are, all too often, past finding out. This should not surprise any of us, after all he is God! (For reflection, Isaiah 55:8-9)

Why does faith have to be so difficult? The answer might very well be found in the very nature of faith. God is supremely interested in growing resolute faith in each of our hearts. Such faith can only grow when the light is dim, when the path is difficult, when all there is, is the Word that was spoken so very long ago. According to the story of Adam and Eve, mankind fell because they had failed to keep the faith in the God they had encountered earlier. In keeping with that tragic beginning, God requires us to relearn to keep the faith in the God we encountered at an earlier time in our lives, who speaks to us through the Word he has given to us. We humans mature as we grow this faith, this trust, this emotional resting in the Creator of our very being and our very soul.

Alexander Solzhenitzyn author of *The Gulag Archipelago* wrote the following when his struggle with God matured to the point of trust, "Bless you prison, bless you for being in my life. For being there, lying upon the rotting straw, I came to realize that the object of life is not prosperity as we are made to believe, but the maturity of the human soul."

He spent 20 years in a Soviet Siberian concentration labour camp for speaking out against the corruption of the communist state.

Quoted in Metaxas, *Miracles,* page 65. *The Gulag Archipelago*, 1918-1956 by Alexander Solzhenitsyn.

Many of the Old Testament Psalms are laments. (e.g. Psalms 12, 25, 27.44, etc.) These Psalms grapple with this human dilemma, keeping these two truths in tension, both the reality of our desperate situations as well as the sovereignty of a good and loving God. Faith that is learning to trust even when it doesn't understand!

It is important that each one of us, too, have our 12 memorial stones to encourage us when our faith journey threatens to falter. During the times when (not if) our faith is stretched then we too can stop, revisit these 12 stones, and find in them the needed encouragement to keep the faith.

What follows are a typical set of 12 stones (my personal set which I keep in my journal) that might be helpful as you collect your own personal 12 stones for your "keep-the-faith" journey. In our world that has so many perplexing variables there is nothing quite as solid and as crisis proof as granite stones!

STONE # 1 – THE JESUS PHENOMENON

According to the gospel records Jesus had only a short 3 year public ministry. He was born and lived his whole life in the most out of the way subject-country of the Roman World Empire. He never wrote anything down for his vagabond group of followers. He never led an army. He never succeeded in any accomplishment that could be considered as having any worldly value. He was completely discredited at his death.

Yet the religion that began on the testimony of this one solitary life, Christianity, exploded onto the world stage within weeks of his death and reported resurrection. Within a few decades it had sprouted in all the corners of the then known civilized world, and this growth happened under the constant threat of violent persecution both from within Judaism, its host culture, as well as from the Roman authorities, the political power of the day. Christianity continues to grow globally today in spite of the fact that it repeatedly needs to weather intense persecution, venomous criticism, blatant internal corruption, and vitality draining cultural compromise.

This amazing historical phenomenon does need an explanation. The one that is frequently made is simply to discredit the accuracy of the gospel stories. Then one needs to ask, who would possibly have invented such a "loser" story that has nevertheless proved itself to be such a resounding historical success? An answer to that scenario may require much more faith than the traditional view.

Another response is to simply categorize Jesus as one of the great spiritual teachers, together with Moses, with Mohammed, with Buddha, etc. To this challenge we simply quote C.S. Lewis's well known response.

"I am here trying to prevent anyone saying the really foolish thing that people often say about him: "I am ready to accept Jesus as a great moral teacher, but I don't accept his claim to be God." That is one thing we must not say. A man who was merely a man and said the sort of things Jesus said would not be a great moral teacher. He would either be a lunatic – on level with the man who says he is a poached egg – or else he would be the devil from hell. You must make your choice. Either this man was, and is, the Son of God or else a madman or something worse. … You can shut him up for a fool, you can spit at him and kill him as a demon, or you can fall at his feet and call him Lord and God. But let us not come with any patronizing nonsense about him being a great human teacher. He has not left that choice open to us." *Mere Christianity*

To put this into perspective, we could anticipate the consequences should someone approach a bona fide devotee of Islam and ask whether it were true that Mohammed had claimed to be the son of Allah, one with him in nature. It is conceivable that this devotee would have denounced you vehemently and then separated head from body for such utter blasphemy. This is exactly what the leaders of Judaism finally did with Jesus for just such a claim, (not by decapitation but by crucifixion).

Before we leave the Jesus phenomenon we need to state that this whole phenomenon rests on the claim that he did indeed rise from the dead. The first disciples of Jesus witnessed this and all but one paid the martyr's price for proclaiming it. During the first three centuries of church history the believers boldly proclaimed the living Jesus as Lord in contravention of Roman rule. "Caesar is Lord" was the required state mantra. Many paid the martyr's price in the proclamation. Through the long years of church history, often so filled with corruption and compromise, we continually read of renewal movements. Each renewal movement was invariably built on the testimony that Jesus was alive and the living inspiration for that renewal. Many here, too, died the martyr's death, often at the hands of the state sponsored corrupt "church".

Many have undertaken the task of collecting the historical evidence for the resurrection of Jesus, for this watershed global event (see Miller, reading list). Repeatedly and unequivocally the Bible record states that everything within Christianity hinges on this one pivotal event.

And if it is really true then all the ultimate questions regarding truth that haunt all the world religions have been settled beyond a reasonable doubt.

STONE # 2 – OLD TESTAMENT PROPHESIES PREDICTED THE JESUS PHENOMENON

The 12 chosen apostles were tasked with the challenge of proving that Jesus was indeed the Messiah for whom the Jewish people had been waiting. The expectation for a Messiah was at the core of Jewish self-understanding. Someone would come to restore their fortunes as a persecuted people. Jesus did not fulfill those expectations. The challenge for the apostles was great indeed.

Many scholars of the old prophecies, contemporaries with Jesus, deduced that there must be two Messiahs that were being promised. One would be a suffering Messiah, the other a victorious, warrior Messiah. Given the desperate Jewish situation under the cruel heavy hand of the Roman Empire, the warrior Messiah was front and centre within Jewish expectations. It was only after the phenomenon of the suffering Messiah that the apostles understood the Old Testament prophesies correctly. There were not two Messiahs, but the same Messiah, who came first to suffer for the spiritual bankruptcy of the people (and of the whole world). It would be the same Messiah who would return the second time as the Warrior Messiah to complete Redemption History. (See Boskey, Chapter 14, *Messiah Jesus: Zion's Stone of Stumbling.*)

The apostles pointed to two major evidences to prove to the Jewish people that Jesus indeed was their Messiah. Jesus' resurrection and the clear evidence of so many prophecies about this coming one were presented to establish Jesus' Messiah-ship. Many Jews did believe. They recalibrated their earlier expectations, and followed Jesus as their true Messiah. The physical restoration would have to wait. (This physical restoration may be in process in our day with the historical phenomenon of the return of the Jewish people to their historic homeland. Stone #4)

Hundreds of Old Testament passages can be cited that describe most of the details of Jesus birth, life, death, resurrection and legacy. His life, as it happened, could indeed be reconstructed from the prophecies about him.

Jesus' birth is described in detail in Isaiah 9:1-7. On the one hand, he is to be a child that is to be born; on the other hand, he is to have the name reserved exclusively for deity. This was a conundrum, second to none, for the "One-God" Jews.

Of course, in keeping with the nature of prophetic literature, the interpretation of these passages could only happen after the fact. During the time of the prophets of old many of these passages must have seemed impossible to decipher. (I find it amazing that the Jews over the centuries carefully kept and preserved these unexplainable prophesies.)

"For to us a child is born, to us a son is given,
  and the government will be on his shoulders.
And he will be called Wonderful Counselor, Mighty God,
  Everlasting Father, Prince of Peace." Isaiah 9:6

His death is described in excruciating detail in Isaiah 53. The significance of this one solitary death could only have been understood after the facts of Jesus life, death, and resurrection had happened.

"Surely he took up our pain
    and bore our suffering,
yet we considered him punished by God,
    stricken by him, and afflicted.
But he was pierced for our transgressions,
    he was crushed for our iniquities;
the punishment that brought us peace was on him,
    and by his wounds we are healed.
We all, like sheep, have gone astray,
    each of us has turned to our own way;
and the LORD has laid on him
    the iniquity of us all." Isaiah 53:4-6

The event of his burial is interesting indeed. Like all crucified criminals his body belonged to the Roman authorities. It was simply to be thrown into the Valley of Gehenna, the city's garbage dump. Here the wild beasts would have done the final dishonour over night. But contrary to the accepted practice, one of the richest men of the state, a follower, in secret no more, had the courage to ask the Roman governor for the body. All of Jesus' closest associates, his disciples, were in such a state of shock, they were unable to act, and if they had tried, would they have been able to get access to the Roman governor to request the body? This rich ruler got permission, took the body and laid it in his own new tomb. A double fulfillment of a seemingly contradictory prophesy! God was sovereign through it all!

"He was assigned a grave with the wicked, and
with the rich in his death." Isaiah 53:9

The historical fact of so many prophecies that so clearly foretold this most remarkable life is a granite stone that we can all lean on when the mystery of our own walk with Jesus is perplexing indeed.

Ultimately, our lives too, like the prophecies of old, will only be correctly understood when we look back from eternity's perspective.

STONE # 3 – THE BIBLE AS A BOOK-FROM-ANTIQUITY PHENOMENON

The Bible, by any measure, is unique in the world of literature from time immemorial to the present.

> It is unique in its authorship – over 40 authors, from all walks of life, over 1500 years, in three languages, yet with one central consistent story line.
>
> It is unique in its circulation and its translation – no other book comes even remotely close to its distribution, as a rule without any official sponsorship.
>
> It is unique in its preservation – No other book has survived so much criticism, so much violence, so much contempt, so much misrepresentation. Yet it has survived to be the best preserved manuscript, accurate beyond compare, essentially 100%.
>
> It is unique in its influence – No other book comes even close to having had such a profound impact on literature, music, art, architecture, or culture as this one.
>
> It is unique in its content – fore-telling prophecies, historical reporting with journalistic accuracy, character studies of integrity (not just the good, but also the bad and the ugly, are clearly presented for its main characters), ethical teachings second to none, and devotional writings that resonate today across all cultures.

Today, in our culture, the Bible is unique in that it is the most available, but for the most part, the least read of all the great books. Indeed it must be so. The only way our atheistic, materialistic, anti-religious culture is able to move "forward" is to silence this book. But history will have the last word, as it has had on so many occasions with respect to this book. Sooner or later this greatest of treasures will be rediscovered.

If the Bible had perchance been lost in antiquity, and if it had only now been discovered and examined then this 2000 to 3400 year old archeological artifact would have rocked the modern world like no other discovery from the ancient or more recent past would have been able to do. The quality of the poetry, the prose, the literature, the accuracy of the historical record, the quality of the preservation, all would have been recognized as without comparison with any literature, any artifact from the ancient past.

> "In addition to illuminating the Bible, archeology has confirmed countless passages which had been rejected by critics as unhistorical or contradictory to known facts."
> Joseph Free quoted in Josh McDowell, *The New Evidence that demands a Verdict,* page 92.

The Bible today is really a book that continues to suffer unjustly. A mere few critics have really taken the time to examine it thoroughly, with an open mind. C. S. Lewis, one critic among many who did examine it, became a believer in the process.

That indeed is a risk that every critic must take!

Errors in the Bible Controversy

There is a lot of scholarship prevalent today whose focus is to undermine confidence in the Bible as a reliable book from history. It must be recognized that much of this 'scholarship from a distance', is driven by an atheistic bias.

Much is made of the many errors in the Bible. The vast

Dan Brown's bestseller *The DaVinci Code* is a work of fiction masquerading as fact. This book's theme — there is a vast global conspiracy under foot to hide the real origins of the Christian faith — makes for suspense filled reading. A great thriller, but to take it as factual is simply misguided. The book harmonizes well with contemporary atheistic sentiment, but not in the least with the best scholarship available.

majority of these so-called errors are insignificant and do not change the realized meaning in any way. Changes in spelling, in replacing words with another with essentially the same meaning, eliminate most of these typos. It needs to be remembered that all manuscripts were copied by hand. (99.9% accuracy under those conditions is beyond excellent. Any comparison with any other ancient manuscripts confirms that.) The few that do change meanings are really not critical because the new meanings are seen elsewhere in the Bible.

In our reading of these critiques we need to realize that atheists have a built-in bias (a view they love) which they cannot escape. They too begin with foundational assumptions. They do not want there to be a God; they do not want the Bible to be true. This bias inevitably colours their research.

Many great analyses of this bent to discredit the Bible by such biased scholarship are available. (Miller, chapter 2, *Can the New Testament, and especially the gospels be trusted?*)

The Bible: a Partnership with God
The few errors that have crept in (they have no effect on the overall message of the Bible) are in keeping with the biblical perspective of humanity. God is ever seeking to restore, and partner with, the image bearer that has been so marred by sin. He continues to trust us to become partners with him for the changes within our hearts and behaviours that we so desperately need. He continues to trust us to create communities that radiate the presence and love of Jesus. He has entrusted to us the spreading of the priceless Kingdom message to all corners of the world. In all of these we see evidence of God's participation, as well as evidence of frail human involvement. Through it all, God is determined to bring everything to its mandated fulfillment.

The Bible follows this same principle of partnering with frail humanity. The preservation of the Bible through its long and turbulent history evidences this so well. We see the human struggle and we see God repeatedly overcoming all the odds. The Bible consistently rises to speak truth to another generation.

How God was able to transmit truth into our broken human family with such a human-involvement limitation, and preserve it for millennia without losing its sufficiency for salvation, is another supernatural phenomenon that should cause us all to pause and reflect.

STONE # 4 – THE HISTORY OF THE JEWISH PEOPLE

According to the biblical record the Jews were God's chosen people, chosen to be the channel through whom the Bible, God's revealed word, has come to us. The Jews were also the tribal family through whom Jesus came into the world. Their culture was uniquely shaped to help us all understand the meaning and significance of that one solitary promised life, the Messiah Jesus Christ.

> The birth of the Jewish state (ca 1500-1200 BCE) is recorded in the biblical books of Exodus and Joshua. This involved the sudden mass leaving from Egyptian slavery and the subsequent rapid conquest of Palestine.
>
> Archeological evidence, or the lack thereof, for these watershed events is shrouded in controversy because of contemporary understanding of the chronology of ancient Middle East history. As a consequence we need to ask, are these unprecedented biblical events historical or are they myth?
>
> The interpretation of the available archeological evidence seems to suggest that our conclusions are shaped by our prior faith position. (Again it seems that the mind is led by the heart.)
>
> A good place to begin an examination of these issues, Timothy Mahoney's documentary *Patterns of Evidence Exodus* © 2015

The fact that there still is an ongoing Jewish presence in our world should continue to amaze us all. It was one of the smallest clans in the ancient near east, the one that has had the most challenging history in terms of conquests and world-wide displacements, the one that has repeatedly survived the greatest of attempts to exterminate them, the one that has survived the greatest of assimilation forces, and the one that has been the most misunderstood of all people. Yet today we see this people-group surviving and thriving in the most difficult of places on the planet. The Jewish people, according to prophecy, are returning to their homeland en masse.

> "In that day the Lord will reach out his hand a second time to reclaim the surviving remnant of his people from Assyria, from Lower Egypt, from Upper Egypt, from Cush, from Elam, from Babylonia, from Hamath and from the islands of the Mediterranean. He will raise a banner for the nations and gather the exiles of Israel; he will assemble the scattered people of Judah from the four quarters of the earth." Isaiah 11:11-12

Their language, all but dead just decades ago, has been rejuvenated. This is nothing short of a miracle, given the fact of 2000 years of exile and diasporas (scatterings).

They have created "an oasis of green in a sea of brown" again according to prophecy.

> "The desert and the parched land will be glad;
> the wilderness will rejoice and blossom.
> Like the crocus, it will burst into bloom;
> it will rejoice greatly and shout for joy." Isaiah 35:1-2

It is indeed interesting to read through comparative lists of people of stature. For example, the list of Nobel Prize winners through the years highlights the blessing that this, in comparison minuscule group of people have been to the world. This is far beyond anything that could have been imagined. Jews make up 0.02% of human population yet 22% of Nobel prizes have been awarded to this ethnic group.

http://www.jewishjournal.com/thebulletinbored/
item/5_reasons_jews_win_so_many_nobel_prizes

Many Bible believing Christians have been forced to reread the old prophecies because the standard interpretations no longer fit. Obviously God is still very much at work in history with respect to this people-group. The history of these people, God's chosen people, is for me evidence that God is active in our world, and that he is determined to bring it to its predetermined prophetic conclusion.

The challenge for us is to become participants in the, as yet, incomplete story that God is writing on the pages of human history.

Of interest to me is the growing interest among contemporary Jews to explore the controversy surrounding Jesus. Many are finding faith in Jesus of Nazareth. A good place to look to find information on this "happening-today" phenomena are two websites.

Imetmessiah.com
joelrosenberg.com see his blog, January 9, 2017 post.

To quote C.S, Lewis in the Narnia Chronicles, "Aslan may indeed be on the move!"

"Aslan, who said anything about safe? Course he isn't
safe. But he's good. He's the King, I tell you."
— C.S. Lewis, The Lion, the Witch, and the Wardrobe.
Drawn by Cristina Bustamante-Araya, CCS grade 11

'A Light in Jerusalem' watercolour by Clyde Williamson.

STONE # 5 – HISTORICAL JEWISH CULTURE, THE FEASTS OF THE LORD

The biblical meta-story has been carved into ancient Jewish culture, and some of this remains to this day among modern worldwide Jewish communities. Moses established seven annual feasts. Each feast celebrated some aspect of the Jewish experience; and after the Jesus Phenomenon it was discovered that these seven annual feasts together were an amazing metaphor for the cosmic biblical meta-story. It turned out that not only Jewish history but the Jewish calendar itself was a prophetic foreshadowing of the grand story that God is accomplishing within human salvation history. The timing and the dates within the year line up beautifully with the Jesus event of history. It is an amazing prophetic confirmation that God really is up to something!

The following is a list of the seven feasts and how they fit into the meta-story. These need to be studied in detail to personally feel the weightiness of the truths that are hidden in them.

Passover: Jesus Death – Jesus has become for us the Passover lamb who takes away the sin of the world.

Unleavened Bread: Burial – Jesus has become for us the Bread of
Life, bread that is without yeast, without sin, a bread that sustains for time and eternity.

First Fruits: Jesus' Resurrection – Jesus has become the first New
Man, the Last Adam, the head of the grace-redeemed people
of God.

Pentecost: Day of Pentecost – The birth of the church, celebrating
the coming of the Holy Spirit who by his indwelling in our
hearts makes us a new creation, one with Jesus and the eternally-
redeemed people of God.

Trumpets: His return – the second coming. Looking forward to
Jesus return when he will complete redemption history and
usher in the New Age in all of its glory, a new heaven and a
new earth.

Day of Atonement: Final cleansing of the cosmos – The beginning
of the end of all the sin and brokenness caused by the rebellion
in the garden so very, very long ago. Sin and Satan are removed,
the curse is broken! All is well! Hallelujah!

Tabernacles: Emmanuel – (meaning God with us), the Kingdom
restored! The relationship between God and redeemed humanity
is fully healed. God tabernacling (living with) his people!

Jesus' crucifixion happened during the Passover feast. His resurrection happened just as the First Fruits celebration was to begin. The
Holy Spirit was given and the church was born on the historic Feast
of Pentecost. The symbolism and the uncanny correlation of the Jesus'
events with the annual feasts must have been so significant as to cause
even a large number of Jewish temple priests to accept Jesus as the promised Messiah (Acts 6:7). These priests sacrificed their historical identity
as the priestly tribe as well as their livelihood within Judaism when they
confessed Jesus as the fulfillment of all that the temple, its sacrifices and
its annual feasts stood for.

STONE # 6 – WORLD CLASS CONTEMPORARY JESUS FOLLOWERS

This stone lists a few of the spiritual giants that have encouraged me on my walk. Young people today have many contemporary spiritual giants to choose from as well.

C.S. Lewis (1898 - 1963) From atheist to agnostic to believer and foremost Christian advocate of the twentieth century. Professor of Ancient and Medieval Literature, Cambridge University, Author of the Narnia children's story series (Christian fantasy at its best – all the stories are Christian apologetic incognito!)

Charles Colson (1931 - 2012) President Richard Nixon's "hatchet man" during the Watergate scandal of his presidency. From prisoner to prison reform advocate and a foremost 20th century apologist for the Christian faith.

Johnny Cash (1932 - 2003) From country music star, through life destroying addictions to a vibrant faith in Jesus – a life redeemed indeed!

Dallas Willard (1935 - 2013) Philosophy Professor, University of Southern California, best selling author of quality Christian literature. His focus as a writer was to help make Christian spirituality real in the day to day for the average layman.

Francis Schaffer (1912 - 1984) Christian philosopher, theologian, best selling author, founder of L' Abri Fellowship, Switzerland, a spiritual resort for young adult seekers after the truth that sets men free.

Billy Graham (born 1918) 20th Century American evangelist, has spoken to millions upon millions of seekers after truth, on most continents, a man of integrity second to none.

Mother Teresa (1910 - 1997) Catholic nun working among the poorest of the poor on the streets of Delhi, India. She and her many Sisters continue to be the hands of Jesus to serve those who have absolutely nothing left to give in return.

Dietrich Bonheoffer (1906 - 1945) Theologian, Pastor, author of
many spiritual-life classics, preacher extraordinaire, political
activist, martyr during Hitler's Third Reich.

All of these spiritual giants experienced both sides of the great divide
(as unbeliever as well as believer) not only personally but through the
many that came to them for counsel. In my opinion, those who have
seen and experienced both sides invariably have more wisdom than
those who have seen only one side.

I am aware that atheists are able to point to many contemporary
Christians who are glaring contradictions to the ideals espoused by
Jesus and his early followers. (All too often I too am one of them, I must
confess.) But then to quote an atheist heard on a random documentary
recently, "There are indeed many foolish people who preach atheism but
that in itself does not negate atheism." That is also true for Christianity.

STONE # 7 - CHRISTIAN MUSICAL PHENOMENA

Handel's Messiah 1741, London, England
At age 56 George Frideric Handel had become a music failure. Handel
had been strongly criticized by the church for writing church music for
the secular opera. The secular public, on the other hand, seemed not to
be interested in his compositions featuring biblical characters. Personally
bankrupt and unpopular, he seemed destined for debtor's prison.

On April 6 of that year he was asked by a wealthy friend and a Dublin
charity foundation to give it one more try. He was asked to write the
music for a collection of biblical passages about the life of Christ.

"Incredible Inspiration

Handel set to work composing on August 22 in his little
house on Brook Street in London. He grew so absorbed in
the work that he rarely left his room, hardly stopping to eat.

Life's Ultimate Questions: Exploring the Stories that Shape Our Everyday

Within six days Part One was complete. In nine days more he had finished Part Two, and in another six, Part Three. The orchestration was completed in another two days. In all, 260 pages of manuscript were filled in the remarkably short time of 24 days."

Christianity .com Messiah and George Frideric Handel

The story is told how Handel's waiter cautiously entered his room out of concern for his health because so many meals left at his door had remained untouched. Handel was found on the floor with tears streaming down his face mumbling, "I have seen Jesus, whether I was in the body or out of it I do not know." He had just completed the Hallelujah Chorus. Ever since the first performance of this musical, everyone, the world over, has stood up when this Hallelujah chorus begins, in keeping with the King's actions during that inaugural performance.

This inspired piece of music has reached the very top echelons of music history. Close to 300 years old, yet it continues to be sung every year during the Christmas and Easter seasons the world over to sold out crowds. During Handel's own lifetime it raised significant amounts of money to help the poor and those languishing in debtor's prison. It is only fitting that it be so, since Jesus Christ, by his own confession, came to set the captives free.

More information is available in *The Spiritual Lives of the Great Composers* by Patrick Cavanaugh, published in 1992 by Sparrow Press, Nashville.

Amazing Grace John Newton, 1725 - 1805
The recent Hollywood film *Amazing Grace* depicts the struggle for the abolition of the slave trade within the British Empire. William Wilberforce, the hero of this true story, was greatly supported by his good friend, John Newton. John Newton himself had experienced a powerful grace filled transformation from abused orphan, to captain of a slave trading ship, to popular village church minister. He wrote many

hymns for the services that he led. His most famous hymn, simply called "Amazing Grace," describes his own conversion from wretched sinner to forgiven beloved child of God.

> Amazing grace! (how sweet the sound)
> That saved a wretch like me!
> I once was lost, but now am found,
> Was blind, but now I see.
>
> Twas grace that taught my heart to fear,
> And grace my fears relieved;
> How precious did that grace appear,
> The hour I first believed!
>
> Thro' many dangers, toils and snares,
> I have already come;
> 'Tis grace has brought me safe thus far,
> And grace will lead me home.
>
> The Lord has promised good to me,
> His word my hope secures;
> He will my shield and portion be,
> As long as life endures.
>
> Yes, when this flesh and heart shall fail,
> And mortal life shall cease;
> I shall possess, within the veil,
> A life of joy and peace.
>
> The earth shall soon dissolve like snow,
> The sun forbear to shine;
> But God, who called me here below,
> Will be forever mine.

A new book has just been published to again help us appreciate the testimony to truth of this amazing spiritual giant and the song that has captured the hearts of so many during the last 200 years. And there is no sign that the popularity of this inspired song is waning. It has become America's most popular spiritual ever!

For further reading: *John Newton: From Disgrace to Amazing Grace*, Jonathan Aitken, 2014.

★★★★★★★★★★★

I have chosen just these two artistic masterpieces for **Stone # 7** from among the many that could be chosen. These two clearly illustrate to me the spiritual dynamic within the biblical meta-story. The one lifts Jesus, the hero of the story, higher, the other mirrors the God-human grace encounter that he came to make possible, available to anyone willing to turn God-ward. Both, after centuries of brightest testimony, continue to resonate within the consciousness of the human heart.

STONE # 8 – CONTEMPORARY FIRST CLASS CHRISTIAN SCIENTISTS

Many of today's vocal aggressive atheists repeatedly claim that science and faith are like oil and water, they simply do not mix. The only way to be a first class scientist is to be an atheist. This claim is simply not true. Many scientists from generations past were committed believers. Many contemporary world renowned scientists are firm believers in the truthfulness of the Jesus story as well.

Owen Gingerich, *God's Universe*, 2006, *God's Planet*, 2014,
Astronomer at Harvard.

Francis Collins, *The Language of God*, 2006, Director of the Human
Genome project, deciphering the human DNA molecule.

Many Christian Scientists have endorsed theistic evolution. God remains engaged, directing and energizing the evolutionary process towards the diversity of life forms we see today. This is worlds apart from classic Darwinian evolution where all life is moved forward simply by accidental mutations and survival of the fittest.

John Polkinhorne, *Reason and Reality: The Relationship between Science and Theology*, 2011, British Particle Physicist, Cambridge, winner of the 2002 Templeton Prize.

Alister McGrath, *Why God Won't Go Away*, 2011, Molecular Biophysics, Prolific author, Professor at Oxford.

Ben Carson (born 1951), American Neurosurgeon, first to successfully separate conjoined twins, joined at the head, quoted as saying, "I don't believe in evolution... I simply don't have enough faith to believe that something as complex as our ability to rationalize, think, and plan, and have a moral sense of what's right and wrong, just appeared."

Paul Vitz, *Faith of the Fatherless: The Psychology of Atheism, Paperback,* 2013, Professor Emeritus of Psychology, Department of Psychology, New York University.

Many more could be listed. I list these because I am, to a degree, familiar with some of their books and articles.

A good question to ponder, "Why do so many aggressive atheist authors neglect to honour this obvious fact: many top scientists are devoted believers as well? Could it be that it really isn't about the truth but about the dominant culture's meta-story that needs to be protected? Are facts that don't fit scientific atheism's worldview conveniently ignored, or worse, argued away?

FAMOUS QUOTES REGARDING SCIENCE AND FAITH

John Lennox, *Daniel: Standing Strong for God in a Secular Society*, 2014, "The more we get to know our universe, the more the hypothesis that there is a Creator God, who designed the universe for a purpose, gains credibility as the best explanation of why we are here." Quoted in Metaxas Eric, *Miracles*, page 33.

University of Oxford's Philosopher Richard Swinburne (born 1934) commenting on the fact that science has thus far discovered about 150 fine-tuned factors (in astronomy, physics, chemistry, biology) on Planet Earth that needed to be "calibrated" just right for earth and the life it supports to be possible, and given the assumption that chance made it so on at least one such planet, many millions of universes with billions of planets would need to be necessary, "To postulate a trillion-trillion other universes, rather than one God, in order to explain the orderliness of our universe, seems the height of irrationality." Quoted in Metaxas Eric, *Miracles*, page 55.

Paul Kalanithi: *Why I gave up on atheism*, published May 27, 2016, FoxNews.com

> Kalanithi now disagrees with the favourite quote of many an atheist, from the Nobel Prize winning French biologist Jacques Monod… "The ancient covenant is in pieces, man at last knows that he is alone in the unfeeling immensity of the universe, out of which he emerged only by chance."

Why? A purely scientific worldview allows no room for meaning, love, fear, hate, honour, beauty, virtue, etc. Yet these are so very much a part of our world.

STONE # 9 – EVIDENCE FOR FAITH AT WORK IN MY OWN LIFE.

When I look back over the many years that I have stumbled along on my discipleship journey I do see that God, the Spirit, is at work. I observe the presence of new appetites, a longing for greater holiness, a longing for closer fellowship with Deity. I observe a growing interest in the Bible, in Christian literature, in Christian music, a longing for anything that provides more significant time in his presence. I observe a continual struggle to overcome the sinful tendencies within my own heart and walk. I observe a longing for greater degrees of victory. I observe an affinity, an attraction to others who share a similar faith as mine, especially to those who too want to grow. Repeatedly I find amazing joy-filled "wow" experiences when I discover new insights with respect to this grand Jesus-Kingdom story.

I suspect that most committed followers of Jesus could affirm the same for their own lives.

I am also sure that modern psychology would analyze the above to death, but then this is one stone among twelve. This stone simply affirms the truth that alongside the historically verifiable stories of Jesus, of the Bible, of the Jewish people, of famous Christians there is also my story. I can point to evidence in my own life that I too am a participant in this much greater cosmic redemption story.

STONE # 10 – PERSONAL ANSWERS TO PRAYER

As a follower of Jesus I too have struggled with many an unanswered prayer (and continue to do so). Somehow, we as western Christians have developed the understanding that God is someone who should cater to our every need and want, all according to our own timeline. Many a personal faith crisis is the result because God has no such agenda. His primary goal is to make us more fit participants in the story that he is writing on the pages of history. As such, because of the conflicts within my own heart; because of my greater interest in the here and now, in the "me, myself, and I" dimension rather than in God's, many of the answers to prayers that I have experienced have been for prayers that I have never prayed. (Many of the things that I am so very thankful for, are things for which I have never even prayed!) In my more sane moments I recognize that it indeed must be so, because as God, he is completely aware of all the behind-the-scenes dynamics of my life, that so often appear to be such a confusing mystery to me.

But more can be said about answered prayer. I can point to some amazing answered prayers that have repeatedly encouraged me. These answers have helped me weather the many prayers that God does not seem to be answering.

Marriage – When my hopes for marriage seemed to me all but dashed, God stepped in and he beautifully orchestrated a complex series of events, that even convinced one reluctant potential bride that this indeed was God's will for us. I could already envision my life as the uncle every nephew wished he'd never had. It was then that God stepped in and made the, to my mind impossible, possible.

I could go on about the lifting of debilitating guilt, the easing of an addictive need to measure up to other people's expectations. I have found assurance that I too am on the faith journey, a child of the King, adopted into the family of God. More practically I can contemplate the successful achieving of a career, and finishing it well, in spite of the many challenges along the way.

This stone, personalized, needs to be in every follower's travel bag. We need to remember that God will often provide these answers to prayers in ways that we least expect. Our challenge is to keep moving forward and to keep our eyes open. God works in mysterious ways! It is all too often only in hindsight that we see the hand of God in our lives.

> "We can only understand life looking back-
> wards, but we must live it forwards."
> Soren Kiergegaard.

STONE # 11 – NEAR DEATH EXPERIENCES (NDE'S)

Modern medicine has created repeated scenarios where people have been brought back from the brink of death. Many have reported spiritual encounters and experiences that are beyond any human earth-bound experiences but that amazingly mirror the faith positions of Bible believing Christians. Below is a short list of biographical NDE's that I have read, that have challenged me to stay the course, to keep the faith, to keep my eyes focused on the prize, till I too have my date with destiny.

> *Proof of Heaven: A doctor's experience with the after life*, by Eben
> Alexander, 2012, Dr. Alexander is a Professor at Harvard
> Medical School. This medically aware treatment of a personal
> experience does not seek to convert, just inform with journalistic
> and professional accuracy.
> *To Heaven and Back: A doctor's extraordinary account of her death,
> heaven, angels, and the afterlife: A true story*, by Mary C. Neal,
> MD, 2011.
> *90 Minutes in Heaven: a true story of Death and Life*, Don
> Piper, 2004.

I am aware of a more recent NDE book, whose authors have come forward confessing it all to be a fraud. It is understandable that some would want to cash in on a phenomenon; that does not necessarily discredit the others. Each needs to stand on its own merits.

STONE # 12 – SAINTS THAT I PERSONALLY KNOW

My own parents – ordinary folk to be sure, yet who displayed a living faith through all the many death defying experiences of their long lives. Born in the 1920's in Stalinist Russia, they survived the great Ukrainian famine of 1932-33 (approximately 8 million Ukrainians perished during this man-made famine). They struggled to survive their teen years during World War 2, not going to school but working very long hours just for the food on their table. Dad was drafted into the retreating

German army in 1943 and survived two years of relentless death on every side as the German army collapsed around him. My parents met while fleeing the Russian armies. They were forced to make an almost impossible, pioneering, new beginning in the "green hell" of South America. Such was the nickname for the Paraguayan Chaco, where the many fleeing Mennonite refugees were forced to settle. They chose to make another completely new beginning as immigrant settlers to frozen Manitoba, Canada, rather than risk more years of relentless struggle in the heat of the Chaco. The only "possessions" to their name during this new beginning were their travelling debts and a string of children whose mouths never seemed to have enough. A most difficult survival story; in spite of this, the first and maybe only song they taught us was *"Gott ist die Liebe,"* - German for *"God is love".* In spite of the tragedy and struggle of their lives, their faith survived and thrived, and they succeeded in passing it on to the next generation. I take my hat off to, and am encouraged by, a faith that is able to mature in the worst of times.

A fellow co-worker –

This contemporary saint suffered a major setback career wise yet was able to forgive, to move on, to put life back together again, and thrive. A living fresh, rich dynamic faith continues to radiate through this wonderful person. This friend is another example to me to stay the course, to keep the faith, through all the struggles and challenges of life.

Men's Prayer Support Group –

As a small group of men we gather to pray for each other and for the church and its mission here in our city. We are all very ordinary, yet there is a growing individual as well as collective awareness that we are participants in something that is global and eternal in scope. Each one, in our own way, needs to meet the challenges of work and family, of paying the bills and getting along. It is in this everyday that we sense a growing longing to not only make our lives fit into the larger biblical meta-story but also for this meta-story to break out of the walls that we have invariably built for it. The Jesus meta-story is, after all, so much more than we could ever conceive and we consider ourselves beyond privileged to have been called to be a part of it, each in our own small way.

This 12th stone is another one that every disciple needs. We are meant to travel together. When (not if) we stumble or fall, the others help in getting us back on our feet. God's preferred way of meeting us is through each other. After all, we humans have been created in his image, and are being redeemed to again be more like him, showing his love and faithfulness towards one another.

Collecting the 12 Stones

In my humble opinion a collection of such 12 stones (personalized to every person's own situation as needed) are the minimum apologetics (defense of the faith) that every new Christian, every young person needs in their travel kit for their own faith journey.

Do not leave home without them!

The ABC Response

We have walked one pathway through the complex world of religion. The whole world is struggling to find true life, a life worth living. Possibly our journey has brought us to the place where we have realized that the life we long for may be found in Jesus. We might be at the place where we are willing to explore how it is that one might find this abundant life, this eternal life, this life that fills the void in our broken, empty, longing hearts.

How do I become a Christian? How do I become a participant in the story that God is writing on the pages of history?

A simple ABC approach may be helpful (**Admit**, **Believe**, **Commit**). The following truths need to be embraced by our hearts and then paraphrased as a short prayer towards God "in whom we live, and move, and have our being." Acts 17:28

ADMIT — We need to come to the place where we are able to admit that our lives are dysfunctional — broken, or simply empty, missing something. Many metaphors could be used. The Bible would simply have us summarize, "I am a sinner, I am not what I was meant to be, I am missing life's potential." (To be a sinner, simply put, means to have missed the mark, not to have measured up to God's standard.)

Second, we need to have come to the profound understanding that this brokenness is the result of our separation from the God who created us. We are at odds with the only source of life. Jesus summarized the Ten Commandments this way:

"Love the Lord your God with all your heart and with
all your soul and with all your strength and with all your mind

and,

Love your neighbor as yourself." Luke 10:27

The first portion, the most important part of all the Ten
Commandments, has to do with our relationship with God, loving him
with literally all that we are. Everything else in our lives flows from this
relational source. This is the relationship that is broken and this is at the
root of all that is wrong in our lives. We need to have come to this heart
understanding – not just a simple superficial nod of the head to this
truth. Maybe more contemplation, more meditation, more self awareness, is needed to develop this heart understanding. (Possibly reflect on
passages like Romans chapters 1 - 3, Psalm 51.)

BELIEVE – Having come to a correct understanding as to the root of
the problem, we move next to the solution. We need to believe that no
amount of education, no amount of enlightenment, no amount of suffering, no amount of effort, nothing on our part can possibly restore
this relationship with a Holy God. The heart change that is needed is
simply too radical, too supernatural, too impossible for us to imple-
ment. The Bible again uses many metaphors to describe it: being born
again, receiving a new heart, breaking the curse, being dead and becoming alive, being blind and gaining sight, being transferred from darkness
into light, being adopted into a new family. All the metaphors underline
the truth that this is something that only God can do in our lives.

This new beginning requires a solution that has a "Made in Heaven"
label. Jesus Christ, God's only son needed to enter our humanity.

- He needed to model for us how humanity was meant to live – in
  complete union with God, a relational dynamic at the core of our
  being (the first portion of the 10 commandments).

- He needed to teach us how to live a life that truly pleases God: all of his words and all of his actions illustrated this (the last portion of the 10 commandments).
- He needed to die for us. The penalty for our sin he needed to carry, the curse he needed to break. (As the God who took on human form, his death is effective for all who confess their sins, who confess Jesus as Saviour.)
- He needed to be raised from the dead so that his new life could be implanted into our hearts. This spiritual life-implant needs to become the new centre of our lives.

This we need to believe. This we need to embrace. This "new life implant" we deeply need to long for.

COMMIT – Simply to believe the above points, simply to accept them intellectually is not sufficient. Jesus came to impart a life that needs to be lived in the here and now, not just in eternity. We need to commit to the Jesus way. We need to accept Jesus as Saviour, and we need to acknowledge him as Lord. Our goal needs to be to live a life that is modeled after his, from one degree of obedience to another. The life-implant he came to bring needs to find release in our lives. Anything short of that may mean that no new life has been implanted.

Christianity has lost a lot of its dynamic today because it has been watered down to such a great degree. Many accept Jesus as Saviour but do not acknowledge him as Lord. Many do the Jesus-stuff on Sunday and forget about him the rest of the week. For many, Christianity has become simply something that clergy live and the rest of us remain mere spectators. For many, Jesus is simply a fire-insurance policy. For many, Christianity has simply become a Christmas/Easter tradition, a box to tick on a questionnaire.

Clearly Jesus had more in mind.

> "Then he said to them all,
> "If anyone would come after me, he must deny himself
> and take up his cross daily and follow me." Luke 9:23

Furthermore, many 'Christians' have substituted a dynamic life-giving relationship with Jesus with a tradition-filled relationship with their church. Instead of true Christianity they practice "churchianity". **Jesus insists we follow him, not an institution**. (Gathering with others who follow as well provides mutual encouragement and accountability.)

A true commitment to Jesus will result in radical real-life changes that will become visible to an ever greater degree. We will notice new appetites; a hunger for God's word, a need for prayer, a joy in worship, a longing to be with other growing Christians. We will notice new struggles; many of the habits that were of no consequence to us earlier will become more and more a source of anxiety until we commit to changing them. We will become aware of a tendency to be more thankful, to have more inner peace and more joy, all heart attitudes that do not so quickly disappear during life's many ups and downs. Above all there will be a growing awareness of the need to work on our relationship with God; the awareness that we are so very dependent on the Spirit who lives within to live a life pleasing to God will grow. Developing this relationship will become the growing passion of our "reborn" lives.

Looking back over our lives, a true commitment will have made a before and after watershed-divide within our personal life's story that will parallel, if not supersede, any of the other great decisions of our lives.

This ABC response, whether it is a process of a minute or one that takes a season, will be buoyed by a faith in God who initiates within us this life-implant that he came to bring, and the life for which we so desperately long. Jesus encourages confidence as we turn our hearts towards our Heavenly Father.

"Ask and it will be given to you; seek and you will find; knock and the door will be opened to you. For everyone who asks receives; the one who seeks finds; and to the one who knocks, the door will be opened." Matthew 7:7-8

The verbs in this passage indicate a keep-on-seeking, keep-on-asking, keep-on-knocking perseverance, a faith that does not give up. A true faith will not dictate but will allow God to answer in his time and in his way. As we pray, as we wait, we begin to walk the pathway of faith. In so doing, we can be sure the seed, possibly completely invisible, has already germinated. The living sprout will be visible soon enough!

POSTLUDE

Many personal issues may stand in our way when making such an ABC commitment. All of these issues may culminate in the most basic of challenges. If we did encounter deity (possibly as that still small voice, as stirrings within our hearts) on this journey that we have been walking, then the only fitting response must be submission to, and trust in, his Lordship. The bending of our wills to an authority higher than ourselves, and ultimately to deity, has been and always will be the root struggle for all of our journeys. Our culture, as a whole, has developed a paranoia towards any kind of authority (from parents to police to institutional to government) and this has complicated our search for deity immensely.

On This Image

IN CONCLUSION – THE END OF OUR JOURNEY
– OR POSSIBLY JUST THE BEGINNING!
Many things could be said by way of conclusion. The greatest encouragement that we could give each other, and we are all on this journey together, is simply to stop, to look towards the heavens, and with open hearts and ears wait for, and call upon, the "Mystery" that in some sense is light years away from us, yet, according to the Bible and the testimony of so many throughout the ages is so very, very close as well.

ON THIS IMAGE SONNET (see next page)
© 2004 by A. J. Mittendorf. All rights reserved.
Used here with permission
Layout by Jordan Bacon

This image, the Hubble Space Telescope's "Ultra Deep Field" (courtesy of NASA), holds 10,000 galaxies in an area the size of the head of a pin at arm's length. With the exception of the five radiating objects, which are stars in our galaxy, everything in the Field is a galaxy. The closest one (lower right) is estimated to be about a billion light-years away. The farthest ones lie some thirteen billion light-years from us. Imaging the entire night sky with the detail of the UDF (Ultra Deep Field Telescope) would require an estimated thirteen million photographs and centuries worth of telescope time.

Life's Ultimate Questions: Exploring the Stories that Shape Our Everyday

In this minutest speck of space reside
ten thousand galaxies—a vast array
of mammoth stellar cities. In each abide
a billion stars, as with the Milky Way,
a hundred-thousand light-years end to end,
a thousand-thousand light-years in between.
Of all the people born on Earth, no mind
could ever conjure such a stunning scene.
But creation's just eternity's façade
made effortlessly by the living God.
And all this, crafted by His fingertips,
shall languish in the smothering eclipse
of His salvation—infinitely more
astonishing than galaxies galore.

Poem: "On This Image" © 2004 by A. J. Mittendorf
Used with permission.
Image: Hubble "Ultra Deep Field" courtesy of NASA and JPL

APPENDICES

A. Living at Culture's Crossroads

B. Recognizing Atheism's Intellectual Strongholds

   Interpretation of History

   Marriage between Atheism and Science

   Separation of Church and State

C. Developing an Awareness

   of our own deeply held Faith Assumptions

Part 6: Appendices

a few thoughts to begin with...

The task of this book has been to help and encourage fellow travelers to stay on the pathway. Hopefully it even challenges some to get back on the path that leads to LIFE as Jesus has defined it.

In the writing of this book it was impossible to stay simply within the parameters of our own personal faith struggles. Repeatedly the culture-wars that are raging in our post-modern countries were brought to the surface. Some would say that our churches have, by and large, given up this culture-shaping struggle, conceded defeat, possibly even joined the ranks of the opposition. Some would say that the church has, to a large extent, simply retreated and focused on private heaven-focused faith within the walls of our church buildings.

Does the strategy need to change? Our media repeatedly reports on contemporary court challenges that have, as a focus, simply the slowing of the erosion of religious freedoms. This focus may be wrong. It implies that humanism / atheism is indeed neutral and simply needs to be helped to see that we as religious people, have constitutional rights that need to be protected. Is this defensive strategy working?

Does the focus need to shift to the offensive? Do we need to challenge atheistic liberal humanism to help it see that it too, is a religion? It too, is based on assumptions, on a belief system, on a cosmic story, that is equally faith-based as every other religion. **Its _neutrality_ must be exposed as myth. Its culture-shaping agenda is religious to the core, and increasingly aggressive.**

Possibly the silent majority can be awakened to take up the cause. That is the only hope within our democratic cultures.

The following appendices have as a goal to encourage followers of Jesus to "contend for the faith" (Jude 3). We need to take up the battle for our western cultures. We, our leaders, need to take these truths into our culture's marketplace of ideas, into the political arena. The eternal destiny of generations is at stake, not just the wellbeing of our countries.

"The best defense is a good offense."

Appendix A:
Living at Culture's Crossroads

In our western world two meta-stories are vying for the allegiance of everyone who has been introduced to, or is trying to live the Christian story.

Secular atheism on the one hand, and Christianity on the other, are in a fight to the death for our hearts and minds' allegiance.

These two stories are at complete odds with each other. We cannot really live them in harmony. If we try, we will live the one **and** merely pay lip service to the other.

Two diagrams may help to illustrate this.

Much of the material for this appendix was first encountered in a Worldview Course taught by Dr. Michael Goheen, Trinity Western University.

See Bartholomew / Goheen, page 196 ff.

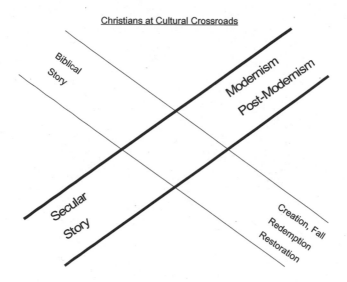

Christians at Cultural Crossroads

Biblical Story

Modernism Post-Modernism

Secular Story

Creation, Fall Redemption Restoration

This first diagram might represent Christians who are unconsciously (or consciously) and increasingly paying just lip service to the Jesus story, to the Kingdom story. They are being influenced more by the surrounding majority culture than by the Christian story. The deeper awareness that these two stories are at complete odds with each other may be missing. The Christian story may provide small devotionals, encouraging moralisms, little sermonettes, weekly traditions, Christmas and Easter celebrations but, by and large, the greater influence in their lives is the culture around them. In terms of life-style, except for the few detours to do the "god-stuff," their lives are minimally different than the population at large. The dynamic of a relationship with Jesus may, for the most part, be missing.

Many of our young people (adults as well) may have left the Christian story possibly because they have become disillusioned with it. Young people are able to see through the emptiness of a shallow tradition. These young people may never have seen or experienced the real thing. So very, very sad.

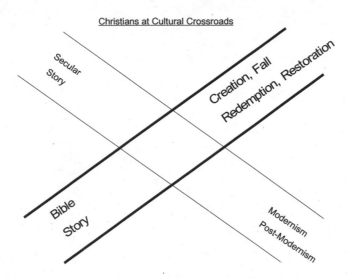

Christians at Cultural Crossroads

Secular Story

Creation, Fall Redemption, Restoration

Bible Story

Modernism Post-Modernism

This second diagram might represent Christians who are increasingly aware of the pull that the majority atheistic culture is having on their lives. These Christians are struggling to maintain their priority commitment to Jesus, to the biblical Kingdom story. They are living in today's secular culture but increasingly are not buying into its values and goals. They recognize and experience increasing tension and possibly even conflict because so much in the surrounding culture is diametrically at odds with the Christian story. Their goal is to submit all their life choices: marriage, career, relationships, entertainment, recreation, finances etc. to the Lordship of Jesus, seeking always to honour him in all things.

These Christians increasingly realize that such a life-style is only possible with a deep devotional relationship with Jesus and in community with like-minded fellow believers. There is a growing Christ-like flavor to their lives. They will increasingly be noticeable within culture as people who are swimming upstream, as living contrary to prevailing culture.

SOME QUESTIONS FOR REFLECTION, FOR DISCUSSION, FOR PRAYER.

1. When does celebrity fan culture or sports entertainment become worship?

2. How do Christian heroes / leaders compare with cultural heroes / leaders?

3. When does today's body culture: fitness, tattoos, jewelry, fashion, youthfulness, etc. become idol worship?

4. When does pursuing the American dream become an idol in our lives?

5. How can an analysis of how I spend my money and/or time be an indicator as to which story I am really living?

6. Parents screen media for family viewing. They screen for adult content, violence and language. Is it just as important to screen media for the underlying cosmic story that is being communicated at subconscious and subliminal levels? Do we need to develop awareness for this message as well? (A movie that struggles with real life issues without any significant mention of God sends a powerful message in support of the atheistic cosmic story.)

7. How would a true follower of Jesus' bucket list compare to the bucket list of someone from mainstream culture? Young people have these lists as well. "Before I settle down to work, marriage and family I want to..."

8. When does attending church just become an add-on in our lives rather than a recharge for living the biblical story for another week?

9. To what extent do our church get-togethers, parties, celebrations, buildings and careers, etc. reflect the values of our secular culture rather than the values of the Kingdom?

10. How do I move from living the one story (secular and paying lip service to the Kingdom) to living the other story (biblical and struggling with the secular)?

Can you generate more reflection questions that should be added to this list?

Appendix B:
Recognizing Atheism's
Intellectual Strongholds

Stronghold # 1
Interpretation of History

Some of the material for this Intellectual Stronghold #1 was first encountered in a Worldview Course taught by Dr. Michael Goheen, Trinity Western University. This exposé (unveiling) of modernism's self-serving interpretation of history strengthened my commitment to the biblical story-line considerably.

History is the interpretation of the facts gathered from the past. Facts such as documents from the ancient past, archeological artifacts, and eye witness accounts are gathered with great care. These facts need to be interpreted. Each interpretation is based on a chosen perspective. Each history has an embedded bias. The interpretation, the perspective, the bias needs to be recognized and must never be confused with the facts. Each history can be an important addition to our body of knowledge of the past.

By way of illustration: Canadian history is being rewritten from the First Nations' perspective, history in general, is being rewritten from the perspective of ordinary folk; each country writes a history from its own perspective, and each historical era has, as well, written a history from its own perspective.

The age of modernism has developed a history of its own era (ca. 1600 – 1960's). This history was written through the eyes of Western European civilization. This interpretation has been the unquestioned "truth" for nearly 300 years. However, influences from the rest of the world are now causing cracks to appear in modernism's interpretation of history.

History is currently being rewritten from many new perspectives, including, and in keeping with, post-modernity's sentiments.

Modernity's "Keys to History": progress through reason, through science and technology, through "European Supremacy," are all being called into question.

For our purposes we need to compare modernism's interpretation of history with Christianity's interpretation of history. The Christian perspective was displaced by modernism's perspective during the turbulent 19th and 20th centuries. Christianity believes that the Bible has the key that unlocks the correct understanding of history. That theme is the coming of the Kingdom of God. (Daniel 2 provides a prophesy of this theme.) This Christian perspective needs to be placed side by side with modernity's perspective.

One intellectual stronghold of atheism is rooted in modernity's interpretation of history. This 300 year Enlightenment's interpretation needs to be critiqued.

A) THE SECULAR STORY LINE

The Thinker – Auguste Rodin ca. 1880
Drawn by Kathryne Rempel CCS grad 2016
Thinking independently: using reason to build a better world.

Interpreting history in keeping with the secular story line.

European history from the perspective of reason — theme of progress	
Age of paganism	pre 400 BCE
Age of reason	400 BCE - 400 CE
Dark Ages / Middle Ages	400 - 1500 CE
Dark, i.e. backwards, middle i.e. not important, medieval means middle These terms are value statements. They are loaded with negative perspective. (The church, the Bible, faith, shaped this era to an ever-increasing degree.)	
Renaissance (rebirth of reason)	1500 - 1700 CE
Enlightenment	1700 – 1800 CE
Modernity	1800's - today
'Modern' implies, we have arrived, advanced, much better. The above three are loaded positive value statements as well! **Reason (humanity) is the hero of the story.**	
Post-Modernity	1960's - today

Is the story breaking down? Is confidence in the modern project (humans using reason to make a better world) losing steam? What will that do to secular humanism's story?

To reflect on as you compare the two interpretations of history: each interpretation is written by the hero of that story: faith (God) on the one hand, reason (humanity) on the other. For the purpose of analogy: how would the hunting story be transformed if the lion were to write it?

B) THE BIBLICAL STORY LINE

Interpreting history in keeping with the biblical story line.

Adapted from Jean-Francious Millet, The Angelus,
The Painting of a Prayer, 1859.
Drawn by Elise Everard, CCS grad, 2016.

Listen for the church bells in the background. Give pause to acknowledge God our Heavenly Father as the Creator, Sustainer, Provider, and above all, our Redeemer.

European history from a biblical perspective	
— Theme is restoring the Kingdom of God (Daniel 2:44 in context).	
Age of paganism	pre 400 BCE
Age of reason — Plato, Aristotle	400 BCE - 300 CE
Redemption initiated – Jesus the Messiah	0 - 40 CE
Judaism's prophetic culture and writings (Old Testament) prepared the world for his coming.	

The church challenges and outlives Greco-Roman culture	40 -400 CE
The church grows – struggles with compromise	400 - 1500 CE
Protestant Reformation — church realignment	1500 - 1600 CE
Age of Conflict — Bible and reason	1600 - 1960's
Church spreads throughout the earth Church struggles to remain true	
Neo-Paganism (see below)	1960's - today
European and North American church struggle with compromise and decline. Globally the church continues to grow, even in Israel.	
Future date – Jesus returns to complete redemption history; to gather in his faith community.	

Faith: God-shaped living: On the surface it might seem that this priority focus on relationship with God would result in an airy-fairy otherworldly panacea. Not so. It is out of, and guided by, this relationship that we pursue all our other activities. It is this relationship that provides the ethical standards, the strength and the critical breakthroughs for all the dimensions of our lives. To the degree that we bring God into our activities, to that extent these become blessings to us, to others, to plants, animals and planet alike.

Neo-Paganism: Me-shaped living:
- The loss of the knowledge of God – people believing what they want to believe.
- The loss of morality – people living the way they want to live.
- Breakdown of marriage, family and clan – this most basic building block of civilization.
- Sacrificing the next generation on the altar of me-centered living (unfathomable national debt borrowed from future generations, environmental destruction – our 'gift' to the future, abortions).

Stronghold # 2
'Marriage' of Atheism and Science - Scientism

Scientific Atheism, it's become cliché! It is assumed that the two belong together, they are one of a kind, they are just so naturally meant for each other, a match made in "heaven". But really, do we need to rethink this 'marriage'?

This 'marriage' has allowed Atheism to ride the coat-tails of Science's tremendous success story. Science has unquestionably made tremendous progress in understanding the world in which we find ourselves. And Science's little sister, Technology, has helped humankind take great advantage of all the wonderful resources within creation. Amazing progress indeed! Atheism has benefited greatly from this 'marriage'. Its reputation has skyrocketed as much as mine would if, per chance, I were "blessed" to be married to a world-class celebrity!

Let's rethink this 'marriage' between Science and Atheism; it may turn out to be a 'marriage' of intimidation!

A) To begin with, it is an historical fact that Christianity and Science had a very cozy relationship with each other in the beginning. Many, if not most early scientists were Christians living within a Christian cultural ethos. They saw so much evidence for a Creator God in the discoveries that Science was making. This continues even to this day; many scientists today are followers of the biblical worldview as well, albeit many in secret because of the mental climate created by the contemporary 'marriage' between Atheism and Science.

Just one website among many that could be listed.

Wikipedia, the free encyclopedia, *List of Christian Thinkers in Science*.

B) Second, the biblical worldview may very well have provided the context for the birth of science-based thinking. The concept of a wise God who created the world with order and beauty suggested a world that could be studied in a meaningful way. In comparison, all the other cosmological stories from the ancient world, suggest only chaos and the wars of the gods as the origin for the world as we know it. As an example, the gods stabbing each other and out of the innards creating the cosmos, mankind appearing as parasites from body tissues, the world as we know it appears. Not much ground for believing that the world might have any degree of order and design to it to make it worthy of study!

> It may be good to reflect whether science-based thinking could have arisen out of a cultural milieu where "accident" explains all that is present today. Evolution's accidental mutations / random events / chance encounters do not necessarily suggest a world that can be meaningfully studied either.

C) Third, Science is limited to the study of the physical world. Atheism, on the other hand, has interests that are far beyond these limits that keep Science from knowing. Science is limited to the study of the material world using our senses, either the naked senses or through the many tools it has developed to observe the raw data that the world provides. Anything that can, as yet, not be observed with our senses and our tools is still beyond the limits of Science. For Science, any claim beyond these limits remains an assumption. Possibly some of these assumptions (hypotheses) may yet be established as fact when an appropriate observation tool or experiment is discovered by some scientist.

Atheism, as opposed to Science, continually pontificates (to make bold proclamations) on issues that are far beyond these limits that restrict Science from knowing. When Atheism proclaims, "Science is the measure of all truth," it has gone beyond that limit. That is a faith assumption. Science cannot take that dictum into the lab to prove it. If Science were honest with its partner it would suggest a logical contradiction. Science might feel honoured by this compliment, but it cannot prove Atheism's confidence in, "Science is the measure of all truth".

When atheists boldly proclaim, "There is no god," they have gone well beyond all the limits that keep Science from knowing. That, too, is a faith assumption (just as much as the "There is a God" claim). Science can, at best, say, "We have not found him (yet)!"

When atheists proclaim, "There is no spiritual dimension (in the traditional sense)" it has again gone far outside

> Evidence for God, that is a matter of perspective. Many of the facts uncovered by Science need to be interpreted; but is the relationship with Atheism restricting free speech? A 'marriage' with serious communication issues!

the limits that keep Science from knowing. Psychology is seeking to understand the so-called "spiritual experiences" of people. But it is next to impossible to study these topics without making a prior commitment. You have to assume that this spiritual dimension exists or conversely, that it doesn't, before you can even begin. Atheism's partner, Science, must really scratch its head as it watches 'experiments' taking place with such a 'just-facts – no assumptions' dilemma.

These are just a few examples where Atheism plays fast and loose with the distinction between fact and assumption, an absolute no-no for Science. Atheism's present day intimate association with Science does not make its many assumptions any more factual than my being in a temple would constitute my being a god!

D) And another friction point, we also hear Atheism boldly proclaim, "There are no moral absolutes, all truth is relative." (an assumption as well). This must really irritate its 'marriage' partner. Science must take great care that it stays within the absolutes of the physical world. Otherwise all spacecraft would miss their mark by galaxies! Science has to play by clearly defined binding rules. Atheism, on the other hand, states that there are no imposed rules; we can make our own as we go along.

As one can see, Science and its present day partner, Atheism, have many serious tension points in their relationship. This 'marriage' between Science and Atheism (Scientism) really does need to be called into question. It needs to be asked, has this 'marriage' even been properly formalized or did Atheism just move in unannounced through the back door? Science, it would seem, would be much better off without this dogmatic roommate. How can Science honestly "keep an open mind and follow the evidence" (one of its core principles) with such an opinionated partner breathing down his neck?

Stronghold # 3
Separation of Church and State

Most western modern nation states have incorporated the concept of separation of church (religion) and state into their constitution, some to a greater extent than others. England still sanctions a state church. The British royal family serves as head of the state Anglican Church but other religions are free to do as they wish. Many nations' constitutions insist on a complete separation between the two.

If our thesis is correct – Secular Atheism is indeed a religion which nourishes the roots for all our answers to Life's Ultimate Questions – then this principle of separation of religion and state needs a major rethink in our day.

The principle of separation of church and state grew out of the context of Post Reformation and Enlightenment thinking within Europe. Essentially all European countries had a state-supported and state-aligned official church. This arrangement gave the state church access to the state's power to subdue all other competing religious groups. Religious persecution of all who did not conform to the state church was the norm. The growth of independent, nonaligned churches was hampered, the freedom to pursue faith as personal conscience dictated was undermined.

The people so persecuted became a significant portion of the first settlers to the New World. The promise of freedom from religious persecution by the state and its official church caused many to risk everything for such a promising new beginning. These pioneers promoted the concept of separation of church and state. It was to be a constitutionally enshrined principle. All faith groups were to have the right to pursue their religion without interference of the state, to even have the blessing and the protection of the state.

> To read from Canada's Charter of Rights and Freedoms:
> "Everyone has the following fundamental freedoms:
>> (*a*) freedom of conscience and religion;
>> (*b*) freedom of thought, belief, opinion and expression…"

http://laws-lois.justice.gc.ca/eng/Const/page-15.html

> And from our neighbours to the South, Amendment I (USA)
> "Congress shall make no law respecting an establishment of religion, or prohibiting the free exercise thereof …"

https://www.law.cornell.edu/constitution/first_amendment

What has happened to this principle today? How is it understood and practiced in our cultures? Today we see religion marginalized within cultures. We see people of faith forced into silence. It is political suicide to identify yourself as a Bible believing Christian within Canada. It is anathema (absolutely unacceptable) to use faith principles to support one's academic, political or cultural positions. All of this, it is proclaimed, in the name of separation of state and religion. As a result, traditional faith has become a private personal matter, just between God and us and generally only within the walls of our church.

If secular atheism / liberal humanism is indeed a religion then it has become the state-sanctioned religion. It has gained complete unfettered and uncontested access to all cultural processes. Culture and all of its institutions, from government to education to justice to entertainment etc., are being shaped by the religion of secular atheism. Morality, definition of marriage, abortion, euthanasia, etc. are all being brought into line with secular atheism's principles. Our society is being reengineered to fit this new state religion.

The very situation that our pioneering fathers wanted to avoid at all cost has returned with a vengeance but most of the population and most of our leaders as well, seem unaware that it has happened: the state wed to the religion of secular atheism, liberal humanism. This religion is using all of the state's power to force everyone into line! Religious persecution is present and gaining momentum!

But most believe that this state of affairs is simply the outworking of the "separation of religion and state" principle. Talk about having the wool pulled over our eyes!

From the biblical perspective it must be seen as Satan's great victory at blinding the spiritual eyes and ears of whole nations. Spiritual warfare is needed if minds and hearts are to be reopened.

Does it not seem that even most churches are falling into line with these new realities with minimal resistance, without any prophetic push-back?

This intellectual stronghold must be exposed; this cultural ignorance must be addressed. Secularism's stance, "We are neutral," must be uncovered as atheism's monstrous self-delusion.

The purpose of this appendix, at minimum, is to help us as Christians become aware of what has happened so that we can stand in the battle for our soul, as well as the soul of our families and friends and, as much as it is possible within our sphere of influence, for the soul of our nation.

Debate and discussion forums need to be encouraged at every level and within every sphere of culture.

Debate topics to consider for these forums.

1. Is every human being religious at the core? Do we all operate on the basis of foundational principles and cosmic worldview stories that we have accepted by faith?

2. What is the relationship between religion and culture?

Life's Ultimate Questions: Exploring the Stories that Shape Our Everyday

3. How is secular atheism just like any other religion?

4. How is the religion of secular atheism, liberal humanism, shaping our culture and controlling our cultural institutions?

5. Which worldview story / which religion inspires the media, the Hollywood empire, the ever-present advertising monster that is channeled unchallenged into our homes? How should Christians respond?

6. Increasingly economic interests are helping to shape reluctant and resistant pockets within society. (e.g. Currently in the news; North Carolina state government is strongly resisting the transgender bathroom laws and in response many global economic interests are threatening to leave or boycott the state.) How should Christians respond?

7. How can the state be neutral in the struggle for true separation of church and state? Can the state remain neutral?

8. How can our Christian leaders speak in the market place of ideas today without causing offence, declaring that their positions are informed by the biblical worldview?

Appendix C:
Becoming Aware of Personal Faith Assumptions

What we believe deep down, really does impact our everyday in everyway.

Use the Ultimate Questions' survey that follows, either as a group, or individually, to develop an awareness of what you really believe. Not only our verbal responses but also our behaviours, our choices, our life rhythms, even our peer group associations need to be taken into account to get a more accurate picture of the contours of our belief system.

We have all subconsciously absorbed a framework for life, a worldview, a religion (i.e. a cosmic story), during our growing up years from those who were closest to us. As we grow older, we encounter many more messages that either strengthen our original framework or that challenge this framework and cause us to move to other positions.

Culture's subliminal, or out in the open, brainwashing processes surround us all. All too often this happens at a subconscious level and we are hardly aware that foundational positions are changing. This subconscious drift or conscious shift continues and becomes more ingrained as we start to act out of the new framework. There may be many indications that all is not well. Inner turmoil or conflicts with family and clan may be indicators that our faith-based life framework needs attention.

The following survey primarily focuses on processing the faith perspectives from Christianity and atheistic secular liberal humanism, the two that are in a fight to the death in your life and mine. All of these statements probe our underlying faith-based assumptions. (Only # 7 is based on historical facts; whether we accept it as historical or not may be dependent on all our other assumptions.)

(Please note, I am deliberately being inconsistent with respect to the positioning of agree and disagree in the following survey. Why I have done this should become apparent at the evaluation stage.)

LIFE'S ULTIMATE QUESTIONS

A) The Question of Truth – The Foundational Question.

1) There is no God to whom we are ultimately accountable. Humanity is the ultimate authority in all things.

Agree   not sure   disagree

2) Religious and Spiritual truths need to be revealed, they are beyond humanity's ability to discern.

Disagree   not sure   agree

3) The Bible is God's revealed word; spiritual truths are illustrated in creation.

Disagree   not sure   agree

4) All religions, if there is any relevance to them, ultimately lead to the same God.

Agree   not sure   disagree

5) Science is the measure for all truth. If science cannot prove a faith precept (i.e. there is a God, there is a spiritual dimension) it is then a myth or worse, a falsehood.

Agree   not sure   disagree

6) The Bible is a story about real people with a real culture, set in a real place, a story rooted in history. God has revealed himself within Jewish culture and history. History is a better guide / a more inclusive guide for truth than science. History can deal with topics like religion and faith and miracle, science cannot, other than to deny them.

Disagree   not sure   agree

7) The Bible provides eyewitness accounts surrounding the resurrection of Jesus from the dead on that one particular day in history so very long ago.

Disagree   not sure   agree

- How does each of the truth layers deal with this resurrection claim: historical, scientific, experiential and religious?

B) The Questions surrounding our humanity.

8) Humans are simply highly evolved animals.

Agree   not sure   disagree

9) Humans are more than just body and soul; we are unique in that we have a spirit, we seek relationship with the spiritual dimension.

Disagree   not sure   agree

10) We have been created in God's image. We are to be a reflection of his moral character.

Disagree   not sure   agree

11) Our lives are evolutionary "accidents" in the universe. Therefore our lives are inherently meaningless. We need to create our own meaning for our personal journey. (e.g. family, wealth, travel, adventure, career, my team, my celebrity, etc.)

Agree   not sure   disagree

- Where does the universal sense of dignity for humans come from? Even the mistreatment of the body of a deceased human is punishable by law in developed countries and frowned upon in essentially all other cultures.

C) The Question of Ethics.

12) There are no absolutes in morals (i.e. no divinely ordained guidelines for what is right and what is wrong) as there are in the physical sciences.

Agree   not sure   disagree

13) Humanity has a God-implanted moral imprint within its soul.

Disagree   not sure   agree

14) Guilt feelings are to our relationships with others and with God what pain feelings are to our physical bodies. (Both can be phantom but both, when correctly discerned, are key to our well-being and survival.)

Disagree   not sure   agree

15) To be mature, to be a truly free person is to be able to do as I ought, rather than as I want.

Disagree   not sure   agree

16) Our cultural concepts of sexuality are simply evolved social consensus, i.e. marriage definition, recreational sex, homosexuality, gender assignment, etc.

Agree   not sure   disagree

17) One man, one woman for life is a religious concept (ordained by the Creator - God).

Disagree   not sure   agree

- How would an ardent evolutionist evaluate today's sexual revolution? What behaviours are conducive to continuing species evolution, which are detrimental?

D) The Questions surrounding Evil and Suffering.

18) Evil is personal. There is a devil and demons, evil spirits who are determined to destroy humankind and creation. The Bible teaches that they are the invisible, behind the scenes, malevolent spirits that often use human agency to accomplish their evil schemes. (E.g. Hitler or Stalin or other "monsters" in contemporary culture are not acting alone, the Evil One is helping, inspiring, possibly even haunting them.)

Disagree   not sure   agree

19) The devil and sin are simply primitive religious con-structs for the inadequacies of our existence.

Agree   not sure   disagree

20) Humanity will evolve out of its present inadequacies. Evolution and science will solve the problems plaguing humankind.

Agree   not sure   disagree

21) All human beings are born with a bent towards destructive self-interest, towards evil.

Disagree   not sure   agree

22) Humankind's tendency towards evil is the result of environment, bad parenting, lack of education, and/or incomplete evolution.

Agree   not sure   disagree

23) Suffering is just a negative that must be eliminated or, if that is not possible, faced grim-faced, stoically. There is no meaning in suffering.

Agree   not sure   disagree

- Why does evil come in waves? (Wars, famines, diseases, social collapses, etc.) It is an historical fact, all cultures eventually do collapse. Will our culture collapse as well or have we evolved to the point where this historical reality no longer applies?

E) The Questions surrounding the Future.

24) There is no life after death. Death is the end of me.

Agree   not sure   disagree

25) There is a Judgment Day. Humans will individually be held accountable for their actions. This is a moral universe. Our human longing for justice is evidence for this future reality.

Disagree   not sure   agree

26) This cosmos operates simply as cause and effect. Death is the end. If I can escape the effects of my choices till death, then I have, to a degree at least, outmaneuvered this cause and effect reality.

Agree   not sure   disagree

27) The seemingly universal and age-old longing for life after death is simply a learned cultural response to our fear of dying or not-being.

Agree   not sure   disagree

28) We all have dreams and longings. (i.e. a better life, making the world a better place, leaving a legacy, life after death, unconditional love, perfect community, etc.) These longings are memories of something lost.

Disagree   not sure   agree

EVALUATION

To the degree that we responded on the left side of the page, to that degree we have bought into the atheistic worldview (liberal humanism).

To the degree that we responded on the right side of the page, to that degree we have bought into the Judeo-Christian worldview.

If our responses are in the center, or all over the place, then our heart-held positions may be shifting. If that is the case then we need to consider; are we shifting our belief system consciously, or by choice, or without our knowing?

WRAPPING UP APPENDIX C

This personal study of what we believe with respect to the Ultimate Life Questions should help us recognize more clearly the meta-story that is influencing our lives the most.

The question then remains, do we really want to live that story or do we need to make some radical changes in our lives more in keeping with the meta-story that we do want to live?

Being aware of our own personal worldview and our core assumptions may help explain some of the behavioural patterns within our lives that may be so troubling to us. There can be no lasting change without understanding and changing the meta-story that undergirds the assumptions we make about these Ultimate Life Questions. This story nourishes the roots of these troubling behaviours.

The meta-story that we do want to live, is best lived in community with like-storied people.

Reading List

Bartholomew, Craig G., Goheen, Michael W. *The Drama of Scripture: Finding Our Place in the Biblical Story*. BakerAcademic, Grand Rapids, Michigan, 2004. This book develops the biblical story and encourages us to find our place in it. This is a readable, yet academic treatment of the Bible as Story.

Dryness, William. *Christian Apologetics in a World Community, Meeting challenges from Naturalism, Eastern Religions, Marxism, Social Sciences, Natural Sciences, the Problem of Evil*. Inter-Varsity Christian Fellowship Press, 1983.

Foster, Richard. *Celebration of Discipline, the Path to Spiritual Growth*. HarperSanFrancisco, 1988.

Foster. Richard, ed. *Devotional Classics*. HarperSanFrancisco, 1993. This is a collection of short readings from a cross section of authors from all the Christian centuries and cultures and walks of life.

Laird, Martin. *Into the Silent Land, A guide to the Christian Practice of Contemplation*. Oxford University Press, 2006. A helpful guide to help calm the mind, connect with God, grow in the spiritual disciplines.

Lewis, C. S. *Mere Christianity*. HarperOne, © 1952. A classic, a "best" book to help get a handle on the basics, by the foremost Christian scholar of the 20th century.

Metaxas, Eric, ed. *Socrates in the City, Conversations on Life, God and Other Small Topics*. Dutton, 2011. A collection of short, easy to read articles that present a broad interface between contemporary Academia and Christianity. Articles are written by Christians who are experts in their fields of study.

Metaxas, Eric. *Miracles*. Dutton, 2014. *Explores* the miracles we encounter everyday, from the one-of-a-kind moon in the night sky, to the uniqueness of life on our planet, to day to day events that defy simplistic explanation.

Miller, Thomas A. *Did Jesus Really Rise from the Dead? A Surgeon-Scientist Examines the Evidence*. Crossway, 2013.

Nicholi, Arman M. *The Question of God, C.S. Lewis and Sigmund Freud Debate God, Love, Sex, and the Meaning of Life*. Free Press, 2003. This is an in-depth comparison of two lives, an atheist and a believer. This book beautifully illustrates the impact that faith and "non-faith" have on life. The author is a professor at Harvard. This book is one of his courses put into book format for the layman.

Smith, James, K. A. *Desiring the Kingdom, Worship, Worldview, and Cultural Formation*. BakerAcademic, 2009. Provides an understanding as to how our modern atheistic culture is shaping us, provides help in deliberately creating Christian culture that encourages faith.

Other Books Consulted

Bennett, Bo. *Logically Fallacious, The Ultimate Collection of Over 300 Logical Fallacies*. eBook.

Blackburn, Simon. *The Oxford Dictionary of Philosophy*. Oxford University Press, 1994.

Boskey, Avner. *Israel: The Key to World Revival*. David's Tent Publishing, 1999.

McDowell, Josh. *The New Evidence that Demands a Verdict*. Here's Life Publishers Inc, 1999.

Parrinder, Geoffrey, ed. *World Religions From Ancient History to the Present*. Facts On File, 1971.

Parshall, Phil. *The Cross and the Crescent, Understanding the Muslim Heart and Mind*. Authentic Media, 2002.

About the Author

Jake has attended Bible College and Seminary, as well as University, seeking to remain a lifelong, reflective learner. He was a Christian School teacher for 21 years. His career included seven years in the public educational system, and short term as a church planting pastor in Bavaria, Germany. He has been married many years. Together with his wife Mary, they have raised four boys; all are doing well in faith, marriage and family, as well as career. Besides the writing of this book, he is presently occupied with the building of their "retirement" home.